D1195366

# The Slab Boys

# THE SLAB BOYS

by John Byrne

Nelson Doubleday, Inc.
Garden City, New York

Copyright © 1982 by John Byrne

All Rights Reserved

CAUTION: Professionals and amateurs are hereby warned that THE SLAB BOYS is subject to a royalty. It is fully protected under the copyright laws of the United States of America, and of all countries covered by the International Copyright Union (including the Dominion of Canada and the rest of the British Commonwealth), and of all countries covered by the Pan-American Copyright Convention and the Universal Copyright Convention, and of all countries with which the United States has reciprocal copyright relations. All rights, including professional, amateur, motion picture, recitation, lecturing, public reading, radio broadcasting, television, and the rights of translation into foreign languages, are strictly reserved. Particular emphasis is laid upon the question of readings, permission for which must be secured from the author's agent in writing.

All inquiries concerning rights should be addressed to Margaret Ramsey Ltd., 14A Goodwin Court, St. Martin's Lane, London WC2N 4LL, England.

*Manufactured in the United States of America.*

THE SLAB BOYS was first performed at the Traverse Theatre Club, Edinburgh, on April 6, 1978, directed by David Hayman, with the following cast:

| | |
|---|---|
| SPANKY | *Jim Byars* |
| HECTOR | *Pat Doyle* |
| PHIL | *Billy McColl* |
| WILLIE CURRY | *Carey Wilson* |
| JACK HOGG | *Robbie Coltrane* |
| ALAN | *Freddie Boardley* |
| SADIE | *Ida Schuster* |
| LUCILLE | *Elaine Collins* |

The New York production of SLAB BOYS opened at the Playhouse Theatre on March 7, 1983, directed by Robert Allan Ackerman, with scenery by Ray Recht (after designs by John Byrne); lighting designed by Arden Fingerhut; costumes by Robert Wojewodski (after designs by John Byrne); and with the following cast:

| | |
|---|---|
| GEORGE "SPANKY" FARRELL | *Sean Penn* |
| HECTOR McKENZIE | *Jackie Earle Haley* |
| PHIL McCANN | *Kevin Bacon* |
| WILLIE CURRY | *Merwin Goldsmith* |
| JACK HOGG | *Brian Benben* |
| ALAN DOWNIE | *Val Kilmer* |
| SADIE | *Beverly May* |
| LUCILLE BENTLEY | *Madeline Potter* |

# The Slab Boys

## Characters

PHIL McCANN:  Nineteen. A Slab Boy. An artist with great natural talent (as yet uncelebrated). Working class.

GEORGE 'SPANKY' FARRELL:  A Slab Boy. Nineteen. From the same background as PHIL.

HECTOR McKENZIE:  Slab Boy and 'runt of the litter'. Nineteen, but small for his age.

JACK HOGG:  Early twenties. A Designer. Very bad skin and hand crafted lumber jackets.

LUCILLE BENTLEY:  Sketcher. Every Slab Boy's Dream.

ALAN DOWNIE:  A new boy.

WILLIE CURRY:  The Gaffer. Scourge of the Slab Room. Mid fifties.

SADIE:  The tea lady. Middle aged. Bad feet.

## *Scene*

The Slab Room . . . a small paint-spattered room adjacent to the Design Studio at A.F. STOBO & Co. Carpet Manufacturers. It is here that the powder colour used by the designers in the preparation of the paper patterns is ground and dished. The colour is kept in large cardboard drums. It is heaped onto marble slabs by the Slab Boys (Apprentice Designers), water and gum arabic is added, and it is ground with large palette knives till deemed fit to be dished. A window overlooks the factory sheds from where the distant hum of looms drifts up. Beneath the window is a sink. Beside the sink are stacks of small pottery dishes (some of them very dirty). There is a broom cupboard in one corner of the room. Rolls of drafting paper, rug samples, paint rags etc. litter the shelves and floor. A large poster of James Dean *(unidentified)* hangs on the wall.

The action takes place during the morning and afternoon of a Friday in the winter of 1957.

# Act One

# Act One

*(The Slab Room)*

*(Enter* GEORGE 'SPANKY' FARRELL *in dustcoat, drainpipe trousers, Tony Curtis hairdo, crepe-soled shoes . . . He crosses to his slab and starts working.)*

*(Enter* HECTOR MCKENZIE, *similarly attired in dustcoat. He is shorter and weedier than* SPANKY. *He wears spectacles and carries a portable radio.)*

SPANKY: Hey . . . where'd you get the wireless, Heck? Never seen you with that this morning . . .

HECTOR: Had it planked down the bog . . . didn't want 'you-know-who' to see it.

SPANKY: Does it work? Give's a shot . . . *(Grabs radio)* Where's Luxembourg?

HECTOR: Watch it, Spanky . . . you'll break it! You can't get Luxembourg . . . it's not dark enough.

SPANKY: Aw . . . d'you need a dark wireless? I never knew that. Mebbe if we pull the aerial out a bit . . . *(He does so. It comes away in his hand)*

HECTOR: You swine, look what you've done!

SPANKY: Ach, that's easy fixed . . .

HECTOR: Give us it. *(Twiddles knobs . . . Gets Terry Dene singing 'A White Sport Coat'.)*

SPANKY: Good God, could you not've brung in a more modern wireless? That's donkey's out of date.

HECTOR: I like it.

SPANKY: That's cos you're a tube, Hector.

*(Enter PHIL McCANN in street clothes and carrying a portfolio under his arm. He sets folio down behind the door.)*

SPANKY: 'Morning, Phil. You're early the day . . . *(Consults wristwatch painted on wrist)* . . . s'only half eleven.

PHIL: Anybody been looking for us?

SPANKY: Willie Curry was in ten minutes ago looking for that lemon yellow you promised but I told him you had diarrhoea and you'd take a big dish of it down to him later on.

PHIL: *(Changing into dustcoat)* Who belongs to the juke box?

HECTOR: S'mines . . .

*(Enter WILLIE CURRY)*

CURRY: Ha . . . there you are, McCann. Where've you been this morning? Farrell there said you were unwell.

PHIL: Er . . . um . . . yes . . .

CURRY: C'mon, what was up with you?

PHIL: Er . . . touch of the . . . er . . . drawhaw.

CURRY: The what?

PHIL: Dee-oh-raw-ho . . . the skitters . . . it was very bad.

CURRY: Why didn't you come to me earlier? I could've got Nurse to have a look at you . . .

PHIL: No . . . it's not what you'd cry a 'spectator sport', Mr Curly . . .

CURRY: In future you report all illnesses to me . . . first thing. How am I supposed to keep tabs on you lot if I don't know where the devil you are?

PHIL: I was down the lavvies . . .

CURRY: You wouldn't get much done down there . . .

PHIL: Oh, I wouldn't say that, Mr Corrie . . .

CURRY: Godstruth, I don't know . . . If I'd had you chaps out in Burma. Diarrhoea? There were men in my platoon fighting the Japanese with dysentery.

SPANKY: How did they fire it . . . from chip baskets?

CURRY: Less of your damned cheek, Farrell. A couple of years in the Forces would smarten your ideas up a bit . . . they'd soon have those silly duck's arse haircuts off you. And what've I told you about bringing that bloody contraption in . . . eh?

SPANKY: What contraption?

CURRY: How d'you expect to get any work done with that racket going on?

SPANKY: Pardon?

CURRY: Whoever owns this gadget can ask Mr Barton for it back *(Protests from boys)* I'll be calling back in five minutes and if you bunch are still lounging about you're for the high jump, understand? Now, get on with it . . . *(Exits)*

PHIL: Chirpy this morning, eh?

CURRY: *(Popping head round the door)* Five minutes! *(Exits)*

HECTOR: My bloody wireless! That was for my Maw's Christmas present.

PHIL: Bless my boater, did you catch that, Cherry? A yuletide cadeau for the squirt's Mater and blow me if old Quelch ain't went and confiscated the blighter!

SPANKY: Christ, Nugent, that's torn it.

PHIL: Buck up, Pygmy Minimus . . . Cherry and I'll think of something. Any ideas, Cherry, old chap?

SPANKY: How about a set of cufflinks?

PHIL: I'll wager that beast, Bunter, had a fat finger in this . . .

*(Enter JACK HOGG with ALAN DOWNIE.)*

PHIL: Yaroo! . . .

SPANKY: Yeugh . . .

JACK: 'Morning, you chaps. Just showing the new lad round the Design Room. This is our last stop . . .

PHIL: Natch. When're you off, Jacky boy?

JACK: Alan Downie . . . George Farrell . . . known to the riff-raff as 'Spanky' . . .

SPANKY: Watch it, Jack. Howdy, Archie . . .

JACK: And this is Phil McCann . . .

PHIL: Hi, Andy . . .

JACK: And last but by all means least . . . Hector.

HECTOR: McKenzie . . . hello.

JACK: This is the Slab Room, Alan . . . where the colours are ground and dished for the Designers . . . you saw the patterns out there. What the lads do, basically, is dole out a quantity of dry colour from those drums over there . . . persian red, rose pink . . .

PHIL: . . . bile green . . .

SPANKY: . . . acne yellow . . .

JACK: . . . dump it onto one of these marble slabs . . . add some gum arabic to prevent it flaking off the paper . . . do we have some gum arabic? Then it's just a matter of grinding . . . *(Demonstrates)* Bit of a diff from the studio, eh?

SPANKY: Why don't you vamoose, Jacky Boy?

PHIL: Yeh, Plooky Chops . . . them boils of yours is highly smittal.

JACK: I'm warning you, McCann . . .

PHIL: Keep away from me! Hector, fling us over the Dettol!

JACK: Jealousy will get you nowhere, McCann . . . just because I'm on a desk.

SPANKY: It's a bloody operating table you want to be on, Jack. That face . . . yeugh . . .

PHIL: You can put in for plastic surgery, you know . . . on the National Health.

SPANKY: Or a 'pimplectomy' . . .

PHIL: It would only take about six months . . .

SPANKY: . . . and a team of surgeons . . .

PHIL: . . . with pliers.

JACK: *(To* ALAN*)* I've just got to dodge down the factory . . . have a look at a couple of 'trials' . . . shouldn't be too long.
*(To* SPANKY *and* PHIL*)* The Boss would like you to show Alan what goes on in here . . . in the way of work.
*(To* ALAN*)* Don't worry, you haven't been condemned to spend the rest of the day here . . . I'll have a word with Bobby Sinclair the colour consultant . . . he could take you through the dyeing process . . .
(SPANKY *collapses into* PHIL'S *arms)*
See you shortly . . . *(Exits)*

PHIL: Get a brush and some red paint, Heck.

HECTOR: What for?

SPANKY: To paint a cross on the door, stupid. To warn the villagers . . .

HECTOR: What villagers?

PHIL: *(To* ALAN*)* Okay, son, what did you say your name was again?

ALAN: Alan . . . Alan Downie.

PHIL: Right, Eamonn . . . let's show you some of the mysteries of the Slab Room. Mr Farrell . . .

SPANKY: Mr Mac?

PHIL: I'm just showing young Dowdalls here some of the intricacies of our work. If you and the boy would care to stand to the one side . . .

SPANKY: Certainly. Hector . . .

PHIL: Many thanks. Right, Alec . . . this here is what we call a sink . . . s-i-n-k. Now I don't expect you to pick up all these terms immediately but you'll soon get the hang of it. And this . . . *(Grabs* HECTOR*)* . . . is what we cry a Slab Boy . . .

SPANKY: You say it . . . Slab Boy . . .

PHIL: Note the keen eye . . . the firm set of the jaw . . .

SPANKY: They're forced up under cucumber frames . . .

PHIL: Note too the arse hanging out of the trousers . . . this last because the Slab Boy, for all he is a special breed . . .

SPANKY: Trained to a hair . . .

PHIL: . . . is expected to put in a full eight hours sweated labour a fortnight for a few measly shillings . . .

SPANKY: . . . and all the gum crystals he can eat . . .

PHIL: Hence the firm set of the jaw. Thank you, Mr Farrell.

SPANKY: Don't mention it.

PHIL: Don't you wish you was one of this happy band, Archie? Grinding out those spanking shades for our designer chappies . . . so that they in their turn can churn out those gay little rugs one sees in our more select stores?

HECTOR: Yeh, you don't know what you're missing . . .

SPANKY: Neither you do, you lucky bastard.

ALAN: I wouldn't mind working in here but they're putting me in with Bobby Sinclair . . .

PHIL: 'Much are you getting?

ALAN: Er . . . three pounds a week . . .

SPANKY: Three pound a week!

ALAN: Round about that . . .

SPANKY: That's more than the three of us put together.

PHIL: Is Waldorf Bathroom your uncle or what?

HECTOR: Old Barton . . . the Boss.

ALAN: What d'you mean? Of course he isn't . . .

SPANKY: Must be some kind of blood relation to start you off at three quid.

ALAN: It doesn't seem an awful lot to me. I've got a kid brother who's earning that and he's only sixteen.

PHIL: What is he . . . a brain surgeon? Three quid!

SPANKY: 'Much d'you get in your last job?

ALAN: I haven't had a job before. I'm at the Uni. University. I've only just left school.

PHIL: Eh? What age are you?

ALAN: Nineteen.

PHIL: Did you get kept back a lot?

ALAN: Stayed on to get my highers . . .

SPANKY: What school did you go to?

ALAN: The John Nielston.

SPANKY: Aw, another one!

ALAN: Oh, did you go there too?

PHIL: No, Albert . . . what Spanky means is you're another one of 'them' . . . a mason . . . or your Old Man is. Place is crawling with masons . . .

HECTOR: Don't listen to them. They're always going on about masons. 'Jimmy Robertson's a mason . . . Bobby Sinclair's a mason . . . Willie Curry's a bloody mason . . .'

SPANKY: He's a bloody mutant.

HECTOR: How come if everybody's a mason you and Phil's working here . . . eh? Tell us that . . .

SPANKY: I lied about my age and Phil there swore to Waldo Bathtaps he'd flush his Nine Fridays down the pan if only we could get to be Slab Boys. Aw, no . . . when Mr Bathtub took me into his office, grasped my hand . . . strangely but firmly . . . and offered me one pound, two and nine a week . . . I went straight home and set fire to my scapulas . . .

PHIL: And don't think it wasn't sore . . . I was there when he done it. Soon as Father Durkin heard we were working here . . .

SPANKY: Phil's Auntie Fay got beat up by the Children of Mary . . .

PHIL: Gave her a right doing . . .

SPANKY: She had to go to Lourdes . . .

PHIL: And the entire family were refused entry to Carfin Grotto . . .

SPANKY: And that really hurt. They were out there every Holiday of Obligation . . . down on their knees . . .

PHIL: Dragging the ponds for money . . .

SPANKY: Having a quick burst on the beads . . .

PHIL: Heh, that's an idea. You ready? *(Together)* In the Name of the Father . . . and of the Son . . .

HECTOR: Cut it out, you pair. Don't pay any heed to them loonies, Alan.

ALAN: But I'm not a mason . . . honestly . . . I don't know what you're talking about . . .

PHIL: Aw, no? Tell us this then . . . When you were in at Barton's office this morning you shook hands, didn't you?

SPANKY: And did it feel like you were in the grip of a man that was throwing a mild epileptic fit?

ALAN: I don't really . . .

PHIL: And did he give your bahookey a pat as you went out?

SPANKY: And said you'd be working with Bobby Sinclair?

PHIL: At three pounds a week?

ALAN: Yes, but . . .

SPANKY: Told you he was a mason!

PHIL: Definitely! First day us poor sods were handed a packet of peanuts and told to report to the Slab Room . . .

SPANKY: Not even a pat on the bum . . .

PHIL: Look at that boy there . . . *(Grabs* HECTOR*)* He was going to be a Capucci monk . . . look at him now.

HECTOR: Hang off! I went to Johnstone High . . . I'm not a bloody pape!

PHIL: No sense denying it, Heck . . . how else would you be in the Slab? Show the boy your knees. *(To* ALAN*)* They're all caved in from praying to St Wilton for a desk.

HECTOR: Don't listen to them bums, Alan . . . they're always going on about getting out of the Slab Room and onto a desk. Some hope. Jack Hogg was four years in here before he even got a sniff of a desk.

SPANKY: There was a lot more designers in Jack's day . . . look at it now . . . Gavin's away to Australia . . . Billy Sproul's in Kidderminster . . . and Hughie Maxwell's got T.B. There's hundreds of desks out there. I'm asking Willie Curry for one . . .

PHIL: Ask him for two . . .

HECTOR: What about three?

SPANKY: Hector, you might as well resign yourself . . . you're in the Slab Room till Miss McDonald down the canteen gets a rise out of her suet soufflés.

HECTOR: I was only . . .

SPANKY: I can see you now . . . unemployable . . . scoffing Indian ink with the down-and-outs . . .

PHIL: Going round the doors with clothes pegs . . . choking weans for their sweetie money . . .

SPANKY: So don't go getting any big ideas about asking for a desk, kiddo . . . you're lucky to be in a job.

PHIL: *(With newspaper)* Lend us a pencil, Spanks . . .

SPANKY: What would I be doing with a pencil?

PHIL: S'that a pen there, Adam? *(Plucks it from ALAN'S pocket)*

ALAN: Hey . . .

PHIL: Gee . . . a Parker Fifty One! What's a slip of a boy like you doing with a pen like this?

ALAN: Just be careful with . . .

PHIL: Aaargh, the nib's fell off!

ALAN: Jesus Christ! That belongs to my Dad!

PHIL: I was only kidding. And less of the bad language, sonny boy . . . a bit of decorum if you please.

SPANKY: That's right, Phil . . . you tell the young turk. Don't think you can let rip with that kind of talk in the Slab Room. We fought two World Wars for the likes of you. That lad there lost a couple of legs at Wipers so the world would be a cleaner and better place . . .

PHIL: Where a man could walk tall . . .

SPANKY: Legs or no legs . . .

ALAN: Can I have my pen back?

PHIL: Ach, I'm not in the prizewinners this week either. Hey, know what the first prize is?

SPANKY: No, what?

PHIL: "First Prize . . . Two Matching Hampsters".

SPANKY: Hamsters? They allowed to give away livestock like that?

PHIL: What're you talking about? "Two Matching Picnic Hampsters . . . Handy for the beach and country walks". No mention of livestock.

ALAN: Pen . . .

PHIL: Here's one . . . twenty three across . . . says it's an 'anagram'. What's an anagram?

SPANKY: S'like a radiogram but not as high off the ground. Give the boy his pen, Phil, you're never going to win it . . .

PHIL: Came pretty close last time . . . three out of forty-eight. I'll win them hampsters yet.

SPANKY: And what're you going to do with them when you do?

PHIL: Cross breed them with ferrets and send them out hunting for Sadie and her tea trolley . . . I'm starving. Anybody got the time? *(Reaches over and tugs* ALAN'S *cuff.* ALAN *takes his pen back)* You'll give yourself a hernia lugging that about, son. *(Referring to* ALAN'S *wristwatch)*

SPANKY: You going to the canteen the day, Phil?

PHIL: No option . . . no pieces.

HECTOR: *(To* ALAN) D'you fancy the canteen? Sometimes quite good . . .

ALAN: Depends what's on the menu . . .

SPANKY: No . . . they don't have a menu, kid . . . s'all chalked up on a big blackboard. There's your Forfar Bridie . . .

PHIL: Hawaiian-style . . .

SPANKY: Your Links Over-Easy . . .

PHIL: Scotch Pie Thermidor . . .

SPANKY: Or if you're really hungry . . . Ostrich in a Hamper.

ALAN: I might give that a try . . .

(ALAN *looks away)*

SPANKY: Healthy appetite, the boy.

PHIL: Aha . . . *(Following* ALAN'S *gaze)* . . . thought those might catch your eye, Albert. *(Crosses to shelf and takes down jar)* This one here contains the mortal remains of one Joe McBride, the oldest Slab Boy in the long history of this illustrious company. Going on for eighty-four was Joe when he got word he was to start on a desk . . . He'd been in the Slab Room man and beast for nigh on sixty year . . .

SPANKY: That's his withered scrotum drying over the radiator there . . .

PHIL: As I was saying, Alma, they eventually put the poor old bugger onto a desk . . . made him a Designer. Of course, the shock was too much for the elderly chap . . . when the cleaners arrived on the Monday morning they found the veteran Slab Boy slumped over his newly-acquired and greatly-prized desk . . . stone dead . . . his hoary old pate in a jar . . . a jar of freshly ground indigo . . . and you know what they say, Arthur . . .

ALAN: What's that?

ALL: When you indigo . . . you indigo!

*(Enter JACK HOGG)*

JACK: Sorry I took so long, Alan . . . bit of bother with one of the jute backings. How're we doing? Lads filling you in all right?

ALAN: Oh, yeah . . .

JACK: Good . . . good. Ready for a recce round the rug works, are we?

ALAN: Sure . . .

PHIL: Mind you don't get lost down there, kid. If you don't get in and out quick the herries eat you alive . . .

SPANKY: Like pirhana.

PHIL: You'll be okay with Jacky Boy though. Soon as they see his kisser all the lassies dive under the looms.

SPANKY: Yeh . . . Big Jinty says it's like somebody smacked him with a bag of hundreds and thousands.

JACK: Just you keep that up, Farrell . . . *(Beckons to ALAN)* just you keep that up. Alan . . . *(To SPANKY)* Don't imagine I'm going to stand here and bandy words with the likes of you. *(Exeunt)*

SPANKY: And don't imagine we're going to stand here and bandy legs with the likes of you, Torn Face!

*(Pause)*

PHIL: Hey, Spanks.

SPANKY: What?

PHIL: D'you think going off your head's catching?

SPANKY: Eh? You mean like crabs or Jack's plooks?

PHIL: No, I'm serious . . . d'you think it is?

SPANKY: How . . . who do you know that's off their head apart from everybody in . . . s'not your Maw again, is it?

PHIL: Yeh . . . they took her away last night.

SPANKY: Christ . . .

PHIL: She wasn't all that bad either . . . not for her, that is. All she done was run up the street with her hair on fire and dive through the Co-operative windows . . .

SPANKY: Thought that was normal down your way?

PHIL: Yeh . . . but that's mostly the drink.

SPANKY: How long'll she be in this time?

PHIL: Usual six weeks, I expect. First week tied to a rubber mattress, next five wired up to a generator.

SPANKY: That's shocking.

PHIL: That's when we get in to see her. Never knew us the last time. Kept looking at my old man and saying "Bless me, Father, for I have sinned". 'Course, he's hopeless . . . thinks it's like diphtheria or something. "The doctors is doing their best, Annie . . . you'll be home soon. You taking that medicine they give you?" Medicine? Forty bennies crushed up in their cornflakes before they frogmarch them down to the 'Relaxation Classes', then it's back up to Cell Block Eleven for a kitbag-ful of capsules that gets them bleary-eyed enough for a chat with the consultant psychiatrist.

SPANKY: Not much of a holiday, is it?

PHIL: Did I ever tell you about that convalescent home my Maw and me went to? At the seaside . . . West Kilbride . . .

SPANKY: Don't think so . . .

PHIL: I was about eleven at the time. Got took out of school to go with her . . . on the train. Some holiday. Place was choc-a-bloc with invalids . . . headcases soaking up the Clyde breeze before getting pitched back into the hurly-burly of everyday life . . . Old-age pensioners, their skulls full of mush . . . single guys in their forties in too-short trousers and intellects to match . . . Middle-aged women in ankle socks roaming about looking for a letter box to stick their postcards through. Abject bloody misery, it was. Dark-brown waxcloth you could see your face in . . . bathroom mirrors you couldn't. Lights out at half seven . . . no wireless, no comics, no nothing. Compulsory hymn-singing for everybody including the bed-ridden. Towels that tore the skin off your bum when you had a bath. Steamed fish on Sundays for a special treat . . .

SPANKY: Bleagh . . .

PHIL: The one highlight was a doll of about nineteen or twenty . . . There we all were sitting in our deck chairs in the sun-lounge . . . curtains drawn . . . listening for the starch wearing out on the Matron's top lip . . . when this doll appears at the door, takes a coupla hops into the room, then turns this cartwheel right down the middle of the two rows of deckchairs . . . lands on her pins . . . daraaaaa! Brilliant! I started to laugh and got a skelp on the nut. The Matron was beeling . . .

SPANKY: About the skelp?

PHIL: About the doll's cartwheel, stupid. Two old dears had to get carried up to their rooms with palpitations and a guy with a lavvy brush moustache wet himself. It was the highspot of the holiday.

SPANKY: What was it got into her?

PHIL: Who knows? Maybe she woke up that morning and seen her face in the waxcloth . . . remembered something . . . "Christ, I'm alive!" Everybody hated her after that.

SPANKY: Did you have much bother when they took your Maw away last night?

PHIL: No . . . they gave her a jag to knock her out.

SPANKY: Eh?

PHIL: So they could sign her in as a 'Voluntary Patient'.

*(Enter* CURRY *carrying a paper pattern.)*

CURRY: Who is responsible for this? Eh? What one of you geniuses is responsible for this mess??

SPANKY: S'not us that do them, Mr Cardew . . . s'them out there with the collars and tie . . . we only grind the colour.

CURRY: That is precisely what you don't do, Farrell . . . and don't try and get smart with me . . . young upstart. Look at this paper . . . just look at it. Feel that . . . go on . . . feel it! S'like bloody rough-cast. Who ground these shades? Or should I say who didn't grind them? This colour's just been thrown onto a slab willy-nilly . . . whisked round a couple of times and dished . . . no damned gum, nothing? It's a disgrace, that's what it is. Mr Barton's just blown his top out there. What do you bunch get up to in here, eh? It's more like a rest home for retired beatniks than a Slab Room. Things were a damned sight different in my day, I can tell you. If we'd tried to get away with shoddy work like that we'd've been horse whipped. Too well off, you lot. Twelve and six a fortnight and we thought ourselves lucky to be learning a trade . . .

PHIL: Oh . . . what trade was that, Mr Curry?

CURRY: Any more lip from you, McCann, and you'll be up in front of Mr Barton's desk before you can say 'Axminster Broadloom'.

PHIL: Oh . . .

CURRY: And that doesn't just apply to you. I want to see some solid work being done in this department from now on . . . d'you hear? I've had nothing but complaints from that Design Room all week. Those people out there are getting pretty cheesed off with the abysmal standard of paint coming off those slabs. And what have I told you about smoking! *(Takes out small pair of scissors and snips off the end* PHIL'S *cigarette.)* Miss Walkinshaw came across two dog-ends in the rose pink yesterday . . . not just one . . . two! What've you got to say to that? Eh?

SPANKY: *(Sotto Voce)* They were meant to be in the emerald green.

CURRY: When Jack Hogg was in here this Slab Room used to be my pride and joy . . . never a word of complaint from the Design staff . . . place was like a new pin. Now what've we got? Bloody mayhem. Jimmy Robertson . . . out there . . . Jimmy Robertson showing Mr Barton a paper . . . contract Persian for Canada . . . held up the pattern . . . his bloody scrolls dropped off. No bloody gum! I want to see a very definite improvement . . . okay? Now, get on with it . . . that colour cabinet outside's half empty . . .

SPANKY: It was half full this morning . . .

CURRY: I want to see those slabs glowing red hot! Or there'll be trouble . . . Big trouble. *(Exits)*

SPANKY: D'you think that might've been a good moment to ask him for a desk, Phil?

PHIL: Yeh, you might've been lucky and got your jotters . . .

*(Enter* CURRY*)*

CURRY: What did you say was wrong with you this morning, McCann?

PHIL: Er . . . Christ . . . emm . . . severe diarrhoea . . . of the bot.

CURRY: If you think I'm swallowing that you're very much mistaken, friend. You were spotted making your way through the gates at quarter past ten. Well?

PHIL: I had to . . . er . . . run down to the factory toilets . . . ours were full up.

SPANKY: That's right . . . Miss McDonald made a mutton curry yesterday . . . even I had a touch of it . . .

CURRY: I'm putting in a report to Mr Barton and you, McCann, are at the top of my list. What little time you condescend to spend on these premises is not being utilised to the full . . . in other words you're a shyster, laddie . . . get me? And you can wipe that smile off your face, Farrell, you're on the report too . . .

SPANKY: What for . . . what've I done?

CURRY: Like your pal there as little as you think you can get away with. Well, I'm not standing for it. That cabinet out there speaks for itself.

PHIL: Christ . . . talking furniture.

SPANKY: I'm not supposed to fill it myself . . . what about them? What about Hector? You've never said nothing to him.

CURRY: Yes, McKenzie . . . I'll see you later . . . in my office. *(Exits)*

HECTOR: Thanks a bloody lot, Spanky! What'd you go and say that for? You're a rotten big bastard, so you are.

PHIL: God, I wouldn't like to be in your shoes, Heck . . . must be real serious. Yeh, Spanks, you must admit . . .

SPANKY: Shut your face. I'm buggered if I'm going to carry the can for the colour cabinet being empty.

PHIL: Half empty . . . don't exaggerate.

SPANKY: Half empty, well . . . s'not my job.

PHIL: But you didn't have to . . .

SPANKY: Shuttup, okay? That's the last time I make excuses up for you.

PHIL: Nobody asked you to make excuses . . . I can look after myself.

SPANKY: What was up you were late anyhow?

PHIL: I already told you!

SPANKY: Aw, yeh . . . your Maw . . .

PHIL: Wasn't just that. She hit the cop with the alarm clock.

SPANKY: They were there and all?

PHIL: They had a phonecall from the manager of the Co about his windows. They knew where to come . . . s' the third time.

SPANKY: She not like the Co-operative then?

HECTOR: We get all our clothes from there.

PHIL: Something about a lovat suit our Jim got. When they got it home it had only one leg on the trousers . . . bastards wouldn't exchange it. Said it was something to do with the nap of the cloth.

SPANKY: What did you do . . . amputate?

PHIL: Jimmucks just had to force both legs down the one trouser . . . gave him a kind of funny mince, that was the only thing . . .

SPANKY: Aw . . . I used to wonder about your Jim . . . that's what it was?

PHIL: He would arrive home from the jigging . . . forty sailors in his wake . . .

HECTOR: I had an Uncle Bertie that was in the Navy . . .

SPANKY: Here we go again. We know . . . he went down with his boat.

HECTOR: Ship . . . 'The Royal Oak'. He was only nineteen . . .

SPANKY: Nobody mentioned your Uncle Bertie, Heck . . .

HECTOR: His photo's on our mantelpiece . . .

SPANKY: We know, we know . . . he was your mother's only brother . . . you've got his medals in the wardrobe and his clothes are on the wall, we know!

HECTOR: It's his clothes that're in the wardrobe and his medals that're . . .

SPANKY: In the bunker, we know . . . we weren't implying nothing.

HECTOR: Just don't . . . he was my uncle.

SPANKY: For God's sake . . .

HECTOR: And he died for his country!

SPANKY: Aw, Christ.

PHIL: Okay, Hector . . . okay . . . I was only kidding about the sailors . . . honest . . . honest. *(Slight pause)* It was forty Sea Scouts!

HECTOR: You pair of stinking bastards! You've no regard for nothing! My uncle went straight onto battleships from the Sea Scouts . . .

*(Enter* SADIE *with tea trolley)*

SADIE: Teas up.

HECTOR: . . . and he was wounded twice before he got killed.

SADIE: Some nice wee fairy cakes the day. What's up with youse? S'that not terrible? Behave yourselves! Come on . . . teas up. And where's my wean? Here, son, come and look what your Mammy's brung you. *(Produces cream cookie)* That's for being a good boy. *(Howls from* PHIL *and* SPANKY)
There's only the one . . . the rest's for the Board Room. I got Miss McDonald to put on an extra one for my baby. D'you like that, son?

SPANKY: Give's a bit, Heck . . .

HECTOR: Gettoff!

PHIL: You rotten sod . . .

SADIE: Leave my beautiful wean alone, you pair of hooligans! You enjoying that, flower? That's the stuff. Now . . . what're youse two wanting . . . tea or coffee?

SPANKY: How come he gets special treatment, Sadie?

PHIL: Yeah, how come? Can me and Spanky not have one of them cookies?

SADIE: I told you . . . they're for the Boardroom. There's fairy cakes for youse.

PHIL: *(Taking fairy cake and banging it off side of trolley)* Fairies been putting cement in them again? Give us a coffee.

SADIE: Please. Where's your manners? Your mothers would be ashamed of youse, so they would . . .

*(Enter* ALAN)

SPANKY: Ah . . . just in time for the chuck wagon, cowboy . . . slip out of them wet chaps and lassoo yourself a wee fairy cake . . . mmm, mmm.

ALAN: I'll take a tea, please.

SADIE: See that? There's a showing up for youse . . . there's what you cry manners. Help yourself to milk and sugar, son. Here, I haven't seen you before . . . you in beside these boys?

ALAN: Er . . . just for the day, I think . . . Jack Hogg mentioned something about Bobby Sinclair . . .

SADIE: Ha . . . you'll be lucky . . . nobody's seen him since V.J. Night . . . *(Quietly)* Try one of them wee scones and butter . . . there's a knife next to your hand . . .

PHIL: Haw, Sadie, you never told us there was butter!

SPANKY: That's not fair . . .

SADIE: Shuttit, youse. And you never put your monies in the tin . . . come on, threeha'pence for tea . . . fourpence for coffee . . . *(To* PHIL*)* Fourpence, I said.

PHIL: I've only got a tanner.

SADIE: I've got plenty of coppers . . .
*(To* ALAN*)* When did you start, son?

ALAN: This morning.

SADIE: Very nice. And what do they cry you?

PHIL: Agnes . . .

ALAN: Alan . . .

SPANKY: Dowdy . . .

ALAN: Downie . . . Alan Downie.

SADIE: Ignore them, son. Look, I'll try and keep you something nice for after dinnertime . . . wee chelsea bun or that? I've got some cream cookies on this morning but they're for the Directors . . . couldn't let you have one of them . . . s'more than my life's worth . . .

ALAN: No, I'm fine, thanks . . .

SADIE: That boy could learn you savages a thing or two. You stick in, son . . . you'll go places. Now . . . *(Takes out book of tickets and purse)* . . . have youse all got your tickets for the Staff Dance the night?

PHIL: Christ, is it tonight? I thought it was next Friday.

SADIE: *(To ALAN)* He thought it was next Friday . . . 'Course it's the night, glaikit . . . don't you try that on with me, Phil McCann . . . I don't see your name down here as paid . . . c'mon, stump up.

PHIL: Have a heart, Sadie, I gave you my last tanner. I'll pay you next month. How's that?

SADIE: You'll pay me after dinnertime or you'll hand your ticket back. Youse boys get plenty. I'll mark you down for this afternoon.

SPANKY: You still going, Phil?

PHIL: Yeh . . . how would I not be?

SADIE: You've got yours, Spanky . . . aye . . . What about you, Hector son? I don't see your name down here. You giving it a miss this year?

SPANKY: 'Course he is . . . his legs would never reach the floor. *(Places empty cup on trolley. Pinches cream cookies)*

SADIE: D'you not want a ticket, darling?

HECTOR: 'Much are they again?

SADIE: Fifteen shillings single . . . twenty five double . . .

(SPANKY *passes a cookie to* PHIL)

HECTOR: I'll take a double.

(PHIL *and* SPANKY *freeze, cookies poised)*

SADIE: What??

HECTOR: I said, I'll take a double.

SADIE: That's what I thought you said, sweetheart . . . D'you want to pay me now or leave it till after?

HECTOR: I've got the money here. *(Brings out two one pound notes.)*

SADIE: Did your Mammy come up on the horses? Thanks son, . . . that's your change. See and the both of youse have a lovely time. What about you, flower?

ALAN: Oh . . . I hadn't thought about it . . .

SADIE: Well you always know who's got the tickets. Is that all your cups? I better get a move on . . . them Directors'll be greeting if they don't get their cream cookies. That's just your money to get, Phil McCann . . . right? See youse after . . .
(ALAN *holds door open)* Aw, thanks son . . . you're a gent.
*(Exits)*

PHIL: Aw, Hector . . . you didn't need to go that far. I know we were giving you the needle but you didn't need to go and throw away twenty-five bob on a ticket just to get your own back. We never said your Uncle Bertie was like that . . . Doesn't run in families anyhow . . .

HECTOR: Not like lunacy . . .

PHIL: What?

SPANKY: He said he knows that. *(To* HECTOR*)* Watch it!

HECTOR: Youse started it.

PHIL: Who're you going with anyhow? Anybody we know?

SPANKY: Yeh, c'mon, give us a clue, Heck. Is it a dame?

PHIL: Or is it her from the Post Desk with the face like a walnut?

SPANKY: C'mon, tell us . . .

PHIL: Yeh . . . who's Miss X?

HECTOR: Mind your own business.

PHIL: It's Miss McDonald from the Canteen . . . right?

SPANKY: Yeh, you're fond of her big cookies, aren't you, kiddo?

HECTOR: Shut your mug.

PHIL: Well, if it isn't the lovely Miss Walnut . . .

SPANKY: And it isn't Miss McDonald with the big cookies . . .

PHIL: Doesn't leave much to choose from, does it? I think it's a kid-on, what d'you say, Spanks? The Big K.O.?

SPANKY: Tell us Hector . . . please. *(Gets down on knees)* Please . . . *(Grabs* HECTOR'S *coat tails)* We're begging you. *(He is joined by* PHIL*)*

PHIL: Put us out of our misery.

HECTOR: Ach, stop acting the goat, will you? If you must know.

PHIL:  
SPANKY: } *(Together)* Yes? Yes?

HECTOR: It's . . .

PHIL:
SPANKY: } *(Together)* Yes??

HECTOR: *(Blurts out)* It's Lucille Bentley.

SPANKY: What????

PHIL: Who????

SPANKY: I don't believe . . . Lucille . . . Lucille Bentley???

PHIL: Lucille would never consider going to the Staffie with you, Hector . . . you're havering.

SPANKY: Lucille and . . . ? Never! He's flipped. Have you seen her, Alfie?

PHIL: She's every Slab Boy's dream . . .

SPANKY: And she wears these . . .

PHIL: Yeah . . .

SPANKY: When did you ask her, Heck?

HECTOR: Well, er . . . I . . . er . . .

PHIL: Where did you get the patter, kiddo?

SPANKY: Yeh, all of a sudden?

PHIL: And she said, yeh . . . just like that?

HECTOR: Well, I haven't actually . . . er . . .

SPANKY: God, our Hector and Lucille . . . phew . . .

PHIL: Our Hector . . .

SPANKY: And Lucille . . .

HECTOR: God, I'm bursting! *(Exits)*

PHIL: Wasn't half hiding his light, eh, Spanks?

SPANKY: Couldn't been all he was hiding . . .

PHIL: Shhhhhh . . .

LUCILLE: *(Sings off)* "Once I had a secret love . . . that lived within
the heart of me . . . All too soon that secret love . . . became impa-
tient to be free . . ." *(Enters)* What one of you greedy gannets's been
in at Miss Walkinshaw's lunchpail? Her sandwiches are covered in
yellow ochre and her orange is glued to her tomato.
*(To* ALAN*)* Hi.
You know she's got a caliper . . .
*(Crosses to sink with waterjug)*

SPANKY: Looking forward to the Dance, Lucille?

LUCILLE: S'there any of them dishrags about? Not the clatty ones . . .

PHIL: *(Producing rag)* Ecco.

SPANKY: You've . . . er . . . just missed him . . .

PHIL: Lover boy.

LUCILLE: Eh?

SPANKY: The pocket-size Casanova . . . he just went out.

PHIL: Wee guy . . . about this height. Give us a look at your shoe.
*(Lifts* LUCILLE'S *foot)* No . . . just wondering if you'd stood on
him . . .

LUCILLE: What're youse talking about now? *(To* ALAN) Honest to God, see when you come in here it's like trying to find your way through the middle of Gene Vincent's wardrobe with a glow worm on the end of a stick. *(To* PHIL) Quit talking in riddles. If you've something to say, spit it out. Who is it you're on about?

PHIL: Hector.

LUCILLE: So?

SPANKY: So . . . you've just missed him. Just letting you know.

LUCILLE: Yeh, thanks. Is that supposed to be significant or am I just being thick?

PHIL: Thought you might've wanted to brush up your foxtrot . . .

SPANKY: Fan down your dangoes . . .

LUCILLE: *(To* ALAN) Can you translate all that?

ALAN: I think they're meaning about you and Hector going to the Staff Dance.

LUCILLE: What?? Me and who??

ALAN: Hector.

LUCILLE: Hector??? Going to the what?? Who's been giving you that guff. What would I be doing going to the . . .

PHIL: You mean he hasn't . . .

SPANKY: The little . . .

LUCILLE: It's the Staff Dance, not the Teddy Bears' Picnic! You mean, somebody actually said I was going with . . .

SPANKY: Hector. Yeh . . . somebody actually said.

LUCILLE: What a bloody insult! I've seen better hanging from a Christmas tree! Hector! Don't make me laugh! *(To* ALAN) Mind and circulate. Sketching Department's straight through . . . you can't miss it. *(Exits)*

PHIL: A right pair of chookies we looked!

SPANKY: Wait till I get a hold of that wee . . .

PHIL: He's for it!

SPANKY: I'll strangle him!

*(Enter* HECTOR)

Aw, here it comes . . . Prince Charming.

PHIL: You shall go to the Ball, Lucille.

SPANKY: What was all that mouthwash about you asking her to the Staffie, you little toley?

PHIL: You had him and me believing you, you . . . She's just been in here.

HECTOR: You never gave us a chance to explain . . .

SPANKY: What's to explain? You led us to believe that you and her were cutting a rug tonight . . .

PHIL: Tripping the light fantastic . . .

HECTOR: I only meant I was going to ask her . . .

PHIL: He was going to ask her . . .

ALAN: That's what I thought he meant . . . that he was going to ask her . . .

SPANKY: Who cares what you thought, sonny boy. You just stand there and model that blazer!

HECTOR: I didn't actually say I had asked her . . .

PHIL: You certainly gave me and Spanks the impression that you had . . .

SPANKY: And that she was champing at the bit to go.

PHIL: She had to ask Fancypants there what one of us was Hector . . .

HECTOR: That doesn't say much for youse either.

SPANKY: It struck a wrong chord with me at the time . . . that a doll like Lucille would want to partner you to the Dance . . . I mean to say, look at you.

HECTOR: What's wrong with me!

PHIL: Everything's wrong with you. Look at the state of the clothes for a start.

HECTOR: There's nothing up with my clothes.

SPANKY: There's nothing up with my clothes. You must be joking. I've seen more up-to-date clothes on a garden gnome . . . you're a mess, Heck.

PHIL: Them duds of yours is twenty years behind the times, kid . . . you never stood a chance of getting Lucille to the Staffie.

SPANKY: Dames like her only go for a guy with style . . . style, that's what counts . . .

ALAN: Don't let them bully you. Your clothes are perfectly all right.

SPANKY: You throwing your voice, Phil?

(SPANKY *and* PHIL *start searching in pockets, cupboards, etc.)*

ALAN: Okay, you've had your joke . . .

PHIL: Aha . . . I've found where the voice is coming from, Spanks . . .

SPANKY: Aw . . . Creepybreeks here. And what d'you know about clothes eh? Look at the trousers . . .

PHIL: And take a gander at the footwear . . .

SPANKY: Aaaargh! What's that on your feet, kid???

ALAN: What's wrong with brogues?

PHIL: You don't really want me to tell you, do you?

ALAN: Go ahead.

PHIL: Well, they're full of holes for a start.

SPANKY: And they look stupid.

ALAN: They're better than those efforts you're wearing . . .

SPANKY: D'you hear that, Phil?

PHIL: Good Christ, man, that's the very boot that conquered Everest.

SPANKY: I thought the sole was wearing a bit thin . . .

PHIL: The Dermot Walsh All British Bubble Boot endorsed by medical men the world over has to be one of the most stylish items of manly footgear on the market and you're comparing them to a stupid looking pair of brogues?

SPANKY: You and Hector's just the same . . . a pair of tubes.

PHIL: Take it from us, you guys . . . youse'll never get a lumber . . .

SPANKY: . . . without this gadgey number . . .

PHIL: It's the finest little boot in all the land . . . What is it?

SPANKY:  
PHIL:  } The finest Little Boot In All The Land . . . taraaaa!

*(Enter* JACK HOGG)

JACK: Would you lot care to put a cork in the glee club? Miss Walkin-shaw's migraine. Thanks. Sorry, Alan, must've taken a wrong turn-ing at the spindle shed . . . find your way back up all right? Listen, I think I've tracked down Bobby Sinclair . . . he's in the Lab if you'd like to . . .

ALAN: Yeh, I would . . .

JACK: Good. You two clowns better watch out. The Boss's on the prowl. I've just seen him have a shufti in the colour cabinet . . . bloody thing's empty . . .

SPANKY: Half empty . . . don't exaggerate.

JACK: Half empty then. Jimmy Robertson's going to be yelling for some crimson lake shortly. Miss Walkinshaw's just upended an entire dish of it over that Alpine Floral she's been working on.
*(To* ALAN) You want to see it . . . what a mess. Six months' work down the toilet. You can have a swatch on the way past.
*(To* SPANKY *and* PHIL) So, that's crimson lake, magenta, olive, cobalt blue, persian red, raw sienna, cadmium yellow, rose pink, French ultramarine, violet and Hooker's green . . . okay? This way, Alan . . .
*(Exeunt)*

PHIL: Did you get all that, Hector?

HECTOR: What came after magenta?

SPANKY: Have you got your dinner suit for tonight, Phil?

PHIL: No . . . I thought I'd go in my old man's dungarees and muffler. 'Course I've got my dinner suit. "Jackson's" . . . Want to get a load of this. White jacket . . . Yankee . . . fingertip drape . . . roll collar . . . swivel button . . . full back . . . sharkskin. Black strides . . . fourteens . . . flying seams . . . razor press . . . half-inch turn-ups . . .

HECTOR: He did say persian red, didn't he?

SPANKY: 'Much is that setting you back?

PHIL: Twenty five and six. Option to buy. Jacket's two quid . . . trousers, five bob. What're you doing, Heck?

SPANKY: Five bob?

PHIL: Yeh . . . guy knocked a half note off them. You can still see the stitches where the truncheon pocket was. You'll do yourself a mischief, Hecky boy . . .

SPANKY: I'm getting mine from "Caledonian" Tailors . . . "Executive Rental" . . . pick it up at six. Guy's waiting on three dozen return from the Orange Lodge in Castle Street. Hoping he's got something to fit me . . . it's my arms, you see. They're three and a half inches longer than my legs . . . or so the Caledonian Tailor guy says. It was him that measured us up. Hard to believe, isn't it?

PHIL: Not really.

HECTOR: Hey, did you really mean that about . . . style? Clothes and all that stuff. No . . . come on . . . kidding aside . . .

PHIL: 'Course we meant it, kid. You'll never get nowhere with those who wear the lumpy jerseys unless you're up to scratch sartorially . . . stylewise. I mean, what doll's going to take a guy seriously in that outfit and with a head like that, Heck?

HECTOR: I can't help the way my hair grows . . .

SPANKY: That's where you're wrong, son. Mr McCann . . . *(Produces large pair of carpet shears).* And don't worry about the clobber . . . we'll organise the alterations . . .

HECTOR: What alterations? No, I only meant . . .

PHIL: You want to go to the Staffie with Lucille, don't you?

HECTOR: I wouldn't mind, but . . .

SPANKY: Then leave it to me and Phil. The togs is no problem. His
Auntie Fay was a tailoress . . .

PHIL: . . . in the Dolls' Hospital. This way, Hector. *(Throws* HECTOR
*over his shoulder)*

HECTOR: Hey, wait a minute!

SPANKY: *(Holding door open)* If you need to give him a friction Jimmy
Robertson's got a lighter . . .

HECTOR: You bastard!

PHIL: To the lavvies!

*(Exeunt.* HECTOR'S *pleas fade off down the corridor.)*

*(*SPANKY *stands for a moment . . . then starts going over the list of
colours in his head . . . )*

SPANKY: Crimson lake, magenta, olive, cobalt blue, persian red, raw
sienna, cadmium yellow, rose pink, French ultramarine, violet, and
Hooker's green . . .

*(Starts working quickly and methodically.)*

*(Pause)*

JACK: *(Off)* Sorry about that bum steer, Alan . . . thought I had him
pinned down for sure that time . . . trouble is that nobody else
knows as much about the bloody biz as he does . . .

*(He and* ALAN *enter)*

JACK: Aha . . . all on your ownio, Georgie? What . . . nobody pulling the strings? Thought Alan here might come back and do another spot in the Slab . . .

SPANKY: The floor's just been mopped.

JACK: I'll leave you to it, Alan. Don't take any snash from these guys. *(To* SPANKY*)* Look, why don't you go through the entire process from the top, Farrell?

SPANKY: I'm busy, Jack.

JACK: Source materials . . . pigmentation . . . texture . . . density . . . all that sort of guff . . . fugitive colours . . . wrist technique. See the way he's handling that knife, Alan? Strain some gum . . . that's always gripping. *(To* ALAN*)* I'd love to show you myself but the Boss has just hit me with a half-drop for Holland. Any problems give me a shout . . . okay? Okay, Farrell? Ciao. *(Exits)*

(SPANKY *works on.* ALAN *watches. Silence)*

SPANKY: Okay, okay . . . you get the stuff, pap it on the slab, water, gum, bingo . . . you grind away till you feel like a smoke.

ALAN: And that's it?

SPANKY: That is it.

ALAN: Fugitive colours . . . all that stuff?

SPANKY: Listen, kiddo, the only fugitive colours we've ever had in here was Coronation Year . . . nineteen fifty three. Six drums of red, white, and blue went missing. There . . . you can use Phil's slab . . .

ALAN: What about texture . . . ? Density . . . ?

SPANKY: Texture . . . seldom varies. Rough . . . that goes for the lot. Smoothest colour we ever had delivered was a poke of mahogany lake . . . lumps the size of Jacky Boy's plooks. Hughie Maxwell broke a wrist grinding a pot this big for Bobby Sinclair . . . him and his wife were going to the Baptists' Christmas Ball as Amos 'n Andy.

ALAN: Density?

SPANKY: Doesn't matter a bugger as long as it doesn't run off the paper onto their cavalry twills. Best to err this side of the concrete scale. Fling us up that daud of muslin . . . I'll strain some more gum.

(ALAN *works away while* SPANKY *prepares the gum* . . . )

ALAN: Phew . . . goes for the wrists . . .

SPANKY: Don't worry, kiddo . . . by the time five o'clock comes you'll have arms like Popeye. No, no . . . too high up the shank . . . *(Adjusts* ALAN'S *grip)* That's better . . .

ALAN: Yeh . . . How long have you been in here?

SPANKY: Too long, kiddo. Be three years this Christmas.

ALAN: That's quite normal, is it?

SPANKY: Nothing's normal in this joint, son. If you mean is that average . . . ? *(Shrugs)* Jack Hogg was four . . . Gavin Dyer, two . . . Hughie Maxwell, six months . . . who knows? Depends if they take to your features . . . how many desks are free . . . how the Boss is feeling . . . what the Berlin situation's like . . .

ALAN: How long's your pal done?

SPANKY: Phil? Year and a bit. Stayed on at school . . . to get his Highers . . .

ALAN: And did he?

SPANKY: No . . . jacked it in. Got sent down for smacking the French teacher in the mouth with a German biscuit.

ALAN: What'd he do that for?

SPANKY: What does Phil do anything for? Laughs, of course.

ALAN: You mean he's nuts . . .

SPANKY: We're all nuts, kiddo.

ALAN: Look, going to cut calling me 'kiddo'? It gets really annoying . . .

SPANKY: Sure, sure . . . anything you say . . . kiddo.

ALAN: Is this about ready to dish, d'you think?

SPANKY: What d'you think?

ALAN: I'm asking you . . .

SPANKY: That's one thing you'll learn in here, Archie . . . don't ask nobody nothing. It's up to you.

ALAN: I think I'll dish it . . . or maybe I'll give it a bit more . . . no, I'll dish it, I reckon. *(He does so)*

SPANKY: *(Waiting till he's finished)* Enough gum in it?

ALAN: Gum? Oh, Christ . . . *(Pours it back onto slab. Accepts dish of gum from* SPANKY *. . . keeps an eye on* SPANKY *as he adds it to paint)* . . . I thought you might be able to add it once it was dished . . .

SPANKY: You can.

*(Enter* CURRY*)*

CURRY: Where's McKenzie?

SPANKY: Oh . . . er . . . Phil had another attack and Hector had to go with him.

CURRY: An attack of what, for God's sake? Not bloody conscience, I trust . . . oh, no . . . not the loose stools again?

SPANKY: No . . . diarrhoea. Hector had to give him a coalie-back down the stairs.

CURRY: Yes, very good, Farrell. You're not too big for a clip round the ear, you know. Give me out a large sheet of paper . . .

(SPANKY *produces a tatty crumpled sheet*)

Is this what you call a large sheet?

SPANKY: S'all we've got.

CURRY: Alan, nip out and ask Mr Robertson for a large sheet of drafting paper . . . oh, and some willow charcoal and a chamois . . . on you go, look sharp.

ALAN: Which one's Mr Robertson?

CURRY: Nylon overall, heavy moustache . . .

SPANKY: S'that not Miss Walkinshaw? Sorry.

(*Exit* ALAN)

CURRY: Have we got any tracing paper in here?

SPANKY: Tracing paper?

CURRY: Tracing paper.

SPANKY: For tracing?

CURRY: Just so.

SPANKY: No.

CURRY: What happened to that roll Mr Barton left?

SPANKY: There's no trace of it.

CURRY: Steady, Curry. How's that gum coming along, Farrell? I take it that is gum you're making?

SPANKY: Yeh . . . there was an awful lot of straw in that last lot of crystals so . . .

CURRY: Probably camel chips . . .

SPANKY: Eh?

CURRY: Dung . . . camel droppings . . . let's have a look . . . yes . . . we used to burn a lot of this stuff under our billies out East . . .

SPANKY: Billies?

CURRY: Billy cans. You were never in the Scouts, were you? No . . . Yes, many's the night we sat hunkered over the old camel dung bonfire after a hard day's trek across the dunes . . .

SPANKY: In the Scouts?

CURRY: In the desert, Farrell. A fountain of bright sparks winging into the velvet sky . . . Some of the lads would hitch up their kilts and get their wee ukeleles out . . .

SPANKY: Dirty pigs.

CURRY: . . . we'd have a sing-song. Yes, those were days. Did I ever tell you about the time Vera Lynn caught up with us? Tommy Christou's Rialto Kinema . . . Alexandria, 1944 . . . *(Hums 'We'll Meet Again')* Here, what's all this business about McCann's mother . . . d'you know anything about it, Farrell? Miss Walkinshaw's got a brother-in-law . . . shop manager in some housing scheme . . . and he was telling her about a carry-on last night. McCann's mother was involved, seemingly. Darkwood Crescent they stay, isn't it?

SPANKY: Er . . . no . . . I think they've moved from there now. They live in Foxbar s'far as I know. *(Inadvertently giving the game away.)* Couldn't've been Phil's Maw that broke the windows . . . must've been some other . . .

CURRY: Thank you, Farrell.

SPANKY: . . . looney.

*(Enter* ALAN *with sheet of paper)*

CURRY: Well done, lad. Have we got something to lean on?

(ALAN *looks around, spots* PHIL'S *folio, hands it to* CURRY)

CURRY: Thanks. Now, let's run over some pointers with you. You too, Farrell . . . you might learn something.

SPANKY: I'm trying to mix up some gum.

CURRY: Leave the gum for the time being and gather round.

SPANKY: You've showed us all that before.

CURRY: You're never too long in the tooth to learn how to execute a floral, Farrell. I'll show you again, won't I? Charcoal . . . ?
(ALAN *holds out a tiny stick)*
Is that all he had?

ALAN: No, he was going to give me the whole box but when I said who it was for . . . and a chamois.
*(Holds out tattered rag)*

CURRY: *(Taking rag between finger and thumb)* I find it difficult to picture this ever making its way sure-footedly up the treacherous slopes of the Matterhorn but still . . .

(LUCILLE *pops her head round the door)*

LUCILLE: Telephone, Mr Curry.

CURRY: Hell!

LUCILLE: Trunk call from Troon. *(Exits)*

CURRY: Don't go away, Alan, I'll be right back. Who is it, Lucille? *(Exits)*

(ALAN *turns over the folio . . . idly looks inside)*

ALAN: *(Taking out drawings)* Hey, these aren't yours, are they?

SPANKY: No, they must be Phil's . . . ho, put them back. If he catches you going through his stuff he'll break your jaw.

ALAN: I'm not touching them. Hey, some of these are not bad . . . look at this one . . .

SPANKY: I'm telling you, Alec . . . *(Crosses to have a look)* God, they are good, aren't they? There's one of Elvis . . . s'dead like him, isn't it? Right . . . shut the folder or I'll get the blame. I get the blame for everything round here . . .

ALAN: Hey . . . how about that red chalk drawing?

SPANKY: That's his Old Man . . . I recognise the ears . . . like Dumbo. And there's one of his Maw. Christ, you can tell, can't you?

ALAN: Tell what?

SPANKY: Nothing . . . tell it's his mother. Shut that folder, I said.

ALAN: Look at the way he's done those hands. Whenever I have a bash at hands they turn out looking like fankled pipecleaners . . .

SPANKY: Which is exactly how your features are going to look if Phil comes back. Get that shut . . . I'm not telling you again.

ALAN: I wonder how he got that effect?

SPANKY: What effect?

ALAN: There . . . The way he's got the nose coming forward from the head . . .

SPANKY: Mines comes forward . . .

ALAN: Some of these are quite accomplished . . .

SPANKY: Aw . . . 'quite accomplished', are they! And what d'you know about it?

ALAN: Not a great deal but anyone can see they're rather good. He's wasting his time in here . . .

SPANKY: Yeh, you have a word with him, kiddo . . . I'm sure he'll appreciate it. Now for the last time, are you going to shut that folder or . . .

*(Enter* CURRY)

CURRY: I've just been having a natter with your Dad, Alan . . .

ALAN: Oh . . . ? *(Tries to gather up drawings)*

CURRY: On the phone. You never let on Bob Downie was your father . . . eh? Godstruth, see you young fellows . . . Chief Designer at Templars . . . ? I'd've been as proud as punch . . . hullo, what's this? Some of your artwork? Let's have a butcher's . . .

ALAN: No, these aren't . . .

CURRY: Tch, tch, tch, tch . . . a chip off the old block, eh?

ALAN: I'm afraid they aren't . . .

CURRY: A right talented pair of buggers . . . I remember when Bob Downie used to work here he was always . . .

ALAN: These aren't mine, Mr Curry.

CURRY: What?

SPANKY: Yeh, they're not his.

ALAN: I was just . . .

CURRY: Who belongs to them then? They aren't yours Farrell, that's for sure. You've got trouble trying to draw water from that tap over there . . .

ALAN: They were just lying around . . .

CURRY: And they can't be Hector's. Too bold for him . . .

ALAN: I think they must be . . .

CURRY: *(Interrupting him)* You're not going to tell me they're McCann's. What's this . . . *(Turns drawing over)* That's the Art School stamp, isn't it? Jimmy Robertson and I used to go up to Saturday morning classes together . . . *(Reads)* "Glasgow School of Art . . . First Year Entrance Exam . . . Nineteen Fifty Sev . . ." what??

SPANKY: Eh?

CURRY: Whose are these?? Come on . . .

SPANKY: How should I know?

CURRY: *(Finding label on front of folder)* "P. J. McCann, 19 Darkwood Crescent, Ferguslie Park . . ." So that's what the loafer's been up to. A flyman, eh? Well, we'll soon see about this . . . Farrell!

SPANKY: What?

CURRY: Away down to the ablutions and fetch that crony of yours up here.

SPANKY: I'll need to wash my hands first.

CURRY: Get a move on! Tell him to drag that miserable carcase of his up those flaming stairs. You and McKenzie can take an arm and a leg each if he can't manage.

SPANKY: And just leave the rest of his body down there?

CURRY: Get those mitts washed! Bloody corner boy. Now, Alan, where were we? Ah, yes . . . now, I'm going to rough in a few roses here. I daresay your Dad's covered some of this ground with you . . . still, no harm in seeing it again, eh? I showed Bob Downie a few tricks while he was with us. Expect he told you, eh? Now, what's the first . . . Farrell, will you gee yourself up a bit! You'd think it was a damned bath you were having! Right, Alan . . . what's the first thing we do when we're starting a charcoal sketch?

SPANKY: Get a bit of charcoal.

CURRY: That's right . . . get the old wrist moving. Make sure it's good and supple before committing yourself to paper. Put those two fingers just there and you'll see what I mean. (Places ALAN'S fingers on his wrist . . . waggles his hand to and fro) Feel?

ALAN: Yes . . .

(Enter PHIL. He is carrying a bundle of clothing which he hurriedly throws into a corner.)

PHIL: Sorry, I can see you're busy . . . I'll call again tomorrow . . .

CURRY: Get you in here, McCann. Bowels back to normal, are they?

PHIL: Eh? Oh . . . er . . . yeh . . .

CURRY: Good. Perhaps you can enlighten us a little? (Produces portfolio)

PHIL: Hey, what're you doing with them drawings? That's private!

CURRY: There's nothing 'private' in here, chum. "Glasgow School of Art Entrance Exam . . ." Well?

PHIL: You've no right . . .

CURRY: Aha . . . not so . . . not so, lad. By the terms of your indentures . . .

PHIL: My what?

CURRY: Your indentures . . . that's what you signed when you started here . . .

PHIL: I never signed nothing! And even if I had that doesn't give you the right to go through my stuff. That portfolio's mine, I collected it this morning.

CURRY: So that's why you were more than an hour late. That diarrhoea business was just a red herring . . .

PHIL: Wasn't me that told you about the diarrhoea . . . it was him.

SPANKY: You bastard!

CURRY: But you went along with it, McCann . . . oh, yes, you certainly went along with it. Thought you had me fooled, eh? Oh, no . . . I smelled a rat right away. So you were up collecting this little lot, were you? Now, don't for a moment think I'm accusing you of being in the least underhand but don't you think it might have been prudent to seek permission before . . .

PHIL: You must be joking! Whose permission do I need? Yours???

CURRY: Or Mr Barton's.

PHIL: Away to . . .

CURRY: Watch it, boy, remember who you're speaking to! Any more of that and . . .

*(Enter* JACK HOGG)

JACK: 'Scuse me interrupting, Mr Curry, but you're wanted in Mr Barton's office.

CURRY: What?

JACK: Right away.

CURRY: Right. *(Heads for door. Stops)* Right! *(Exits)*

PHIL: The little . . . ! Did you hear it?? His permission?? His bloody
. . . ?

SPANKY: You didn't need to shop us like that, did you?

PHIL: What?

SPANKY: I was only trying to stop you getting into trouble. Some
thanks I get.

PHIL: What're you talking about?

SPANKY: The dia-bloody-rrhoea. "It was him". Thanks a bloody lot!

PHIL: That isn't important. Did you hear what that little keech was
saying about me going to Art School?

JACK: So that's what all the racket was about?

PHIL: Yeh . . . Curry was making out I was being devious cos I wanted
to get out of here . . .

SPANKY: Well, I never knew nothing about it either.

PHIL: I don't have to tell you everything, do I?

SPANKY: You told us about your Maw . . .

*(Pause)*

JACK: It's a pretty tough entrance exam, you know. I've tried it . . .

PHIL: Who asked you? You can't even get the tin trunks off a chocolate
soldier, Jack.

JACK: Hey . . . wait a minute . . .

SPANKY: Yeh, the boy was only saying . . .

PHIL: I knew you'd turn on us, ya whore! I bet you it was you showed Hitler my folio.

SPANKY: It was not!

ALAN: It was me, if you must know, and I didn't do it deliberately . . .

SPANKY: I warned him to leave it alone . . . didn't I, Archie?

JACK: I don't see what all the fuss is about anyway. Time enough when the results come out. I've got a friend sat the exam and she says you don't hear till next month . . . you get notified by post . . .

PHIL: Bully for her. Well, I'll be hearing sooner than that, Jacky Boy . . . in fact, I'll know by this afternoon . . . so there.

SPANKY: How come? If Jack's china doesn't get word till . . .

PHIL: Doll in the Art School said she'd give us a ring . . . gave her the number . . .

SPANKY: This number?

PHIL: Used a bit of the old charm . . .

SPANKY: Don't see Willie passing on any messages. Doesn't let any of us get personal calls unless it's a matter of life and death . . .

PHIL: Told her to say it was the hospital . . .

JACK: That's a bit off. Other people have to wait on their letters . . .

PHIL: I'm not other people, Jack.

JACK: How about that, Alan?

PHIL: *(To* ALAN) You open your mouth and your head's going down it!

JACK: Hey . . . hey . . .

PHIL: Piss off, Pimple Chops . . . away back to your desk and fester.

ALAN: It's all right, Jack . . .

JACK: It's just as well for you I'm on a rush job, McCann. *(Exits)*

ALAN: All he was saying was it's a difficult exam . . .

SPANKY: There's that voice again . . .

PHIL: Difficult? It was a cakewalk, kiddo. All this dame has to do is pick up the phone . . . give us the nod.

ALAN: I hope you're right . . . *(Exits)*

PHIL: Of course I'm right!

SPANKY: It'll blow over, Phil . . . you know what Curry's like . . .

*(Enter* CURRY)

CURRY: Did McKenzie come up with you, McCann? *(To* SPANKY) Did McKenzie come up with him?

(SPANKY *shrugs)*

Well, tell him to come to my office the moment he appears. *(Exits)*

SPANKY: See? It's Hector he's got it in for . . . not you. You and me gets off light compared to Heck. That's the second time he's asked to see him today.

PHIL: What d'you think? His cards?

SPANKY: What d'you think?

PHIL: Where is he anyhow?

SPANKY: Who?

PHIL: Hector.

SPANKY: Thought he was down the bog along with you?

PHIL: Yeh . . . but he managed to get free.

SPANKY: Free?

PHIL: I had him tied to a radiator but he must've chewed through the ropes while I was having a . . .

SPANKY: You mean he's wandering about without a stitch??

PHIL: He's got his simmit on . . . that didn't need restyling.

SPANKY: He'll get bloody frostbite, ya swine. How could you do that to him?

PHIL: It was your idea and all, don't forget.

SPANKY: How're we going to find him?

PHIL: Easy. Follow the trail of blood.

SPANKY: Blood? You never beat him up as well, ya pig!

PHIL: I gave his ear a nick with the shears while I was trimming his hair . . .

SPANKY: You're a bloody sadist, Phil.

PHIL: I was trying to get the boy a date with Lucille.

SPANKY: Yeh . . . some chance he's got now. Who'd want to go to the Staffie with a one-eared, baldy-headed midget in a blood-stained simmit!!? No, come on, Phil . . . we better do something.

PHIL: We'll do what we were going to do in the first place . . . get his clothes restyled.

SPANKY: D'you think that's wise?

PHIL: Listen, you know how much this means to Heck . . . getting a date with Lucille. I mean, to you and me she's just a bit of stuff . . .

SPANKY: Some bit of stuff . . .

PHIL: Yeh, but to Hector she is "It" . . . the Real Thing . . . The Empire State . . . Niagara Falls . . .

SPANKY: The thrupenny in the Dumpling.

PHIL: Exactly. It's the least we can do. What're you laughing at, ya dog? You don't reckon Heck's sophisticated enough to get his loins in a fankle over a dame? *(Holds up* HECTOR'S *shirt)* What d'you think . . . a Billy Eckstein . . . or a Dennis Lotis?

SPANKY: What about an Eve Boswell?

PHIL: It would mean a pretty drastic job with the shears.

SPANKY: Yeh, best just stick to altering the togs.

*(Lunchtime hooter sounds. Enter* ALAN.)

ALAN: Is that lunchtime?

PHIL: No . . . It's dinnertime creep, and don't think you're sitting beside us . . . The grub's enough to put you off your dinner. *(To* SPANKY) Last one down the canteen's a Designer!

SPANKY: Hurrraaaaaaaaaaaaaaay!

*(Exeunt.* ALAN *is left standing in the middle of the room. Then he too exits.)*

*(Curtain.)*

# Act Two

# Act Two

*(The Afternoon)*

*(Enter* PHIL. *He crosses to folio, starts sorting out his drawings)*

*(Enter* SPANKY*)*

SPANKY: God, that dinner was revolting . . .

PHIL: I told you not to have the salmonella on toast.

SPANKY: I think I'm going to be sick.

PHIL: Well, don't hang over the shades . . . there's gum in them already. *(He lights up cigarette)*

*(Enter* ALAN*)*

ALAN: Quite a nice lunch they do.

*(Silence)*

Bobby Sinclair's tied up with some problem hanks at the moment so I thought I might come and do some grinding.

*(Silence)*

What's wrong with that? Mr Curry certainly thought I could do a bit.

*(Silence)*

I don't mind . . . I'll just go and let Mr Curry know I'm not needed . . .

*(Heads for door)*

SPANKY: Hold on, Archie. Here . . .

*(Indicates slab)*

ALAN: I want to learn as much as possible while I'm here. *(Takes up palette knife)*

PHIL: You haven't been drinking, have you?

SPANKY: Look at this, Phil . . . boy's a natural. Look at the way the calf muscles are bulging out on the back of his neck. When you've finished that there's some Hunting Stewart there . . .

ALAN: Thanks . . .

SPANKY: Me and Phil'll lie over here and watch you for a bit . . . okay?

PHIL: Ask him if he wants a drag . . . ?

ALAN: I don't smoke.

*(Enter CURRY quietly)*

PHIL: ⎫
SPANKY: ⎭ *(Together)* Surprise, surprise!

CURRY: Surprise, surprise! Young Downie working away and you two Teddy Boys lounging back having a puff. On your pins! Douse them smokes and let's be having you! Come on, jump to it! Finding it difficult to get up, McCann? What do they do . . . spray those trousers on? Or don't you take them off, is that the secret? Give him a hand, Farrell, for God's sake or we'll be here all day. I don't know . . . if you'd seen those P.O.W.s breaking their backs on the Burma

Road . . . young chaps . . . age of yourselves . . . dropping like flies
. . . beri-beri . . . cholera . . . you name it . . .

PHIL: Windypops?

CURRY: Not a peep out of them. Scabbing away like billy-o rather than give in. Get those palette knives in your mitts, quick as you like, Farrell. You too, McCann . . . at the double! Alan, drag yourself away for a mo. Right, you pair, see if you can't do half as well as this young fellow. Come on, Farrell, don't just stand there like G.I. Joe with a pocketfull of nylons, waiting for a pick-up . . . get on with it. This way, Alan . . . Mr Barton's laid out some pre-war pattern books for us . . .

*(Exeunt)*

PHIL: "My Forty Years Giving The Japs Merry Gyp" . . . The Memoirs of Jungle Jim.

SPANKY: Japs, my arse. Jimmy Robertson told me Willie was a typist in the Pay Corps. Nearest he ever got to Burma was the Bamboo Tea Lounge in Incle Street.

PHIL: He's a wee blowhard . . . he doesn't scare me.

SPANKY: Lookout!

*(Enter JACK HOGG. He has a bundle of mags)*

JACK: Alan around?

PHIL: Tall fat guy with scarlet fever and his nose in a sling?

JACK: Just tell him I've got those mags he asked about . . .

SPANKY: What mags are these, Jacky Boy?

PHIL: Yeh . . . how come we never get to see them?

SPANKY: Yeh . . . how come?

JACK: They're about design . . . I shouldn't think you'd be remotely
interested . . .

PHIL: Oh, is that right? Tell him, Spanks . . . are we interested?

SPANKY: Not really.

PHIL: So you think twice before lurching in here and accusing the
brother and me of not giving a monkey's. The designing of carpets for
the hoi polloi may mean nothing to you, Hogg, but it means a damn
sight less to us. Right, Spanky?

SPANKY: Roger.

PHIL: Sorry . . . Roger.

JACK: You're so smart, aren't you? So bloody smart, the pair of you.
You're just pea green if anyone takes an interest in things . . .

SPANKY: Pea green? That's a new one . . .

JACK: You nobbled Hector when he first started, didn't you? He used to
come out to my desk, we'd go through some carpet mags together
. . . but, oh no, you soon put a stop to that . . . called him for
everything . . . made his life a misery. A pair of bullyboys, that's
what you are. Hector could've been a pretty good designer by now
. . . yes, he could! Better than either of you, anyway. When was the
last time you were down the Showroom . . . eh? Neither of you takes
the least interest in any trials that come up. In fact, I bet you don't
even know what any of us is working on out there . . .

PHIL: *(Producing tatty piece of carpet)* Fourteen and eleven the square
furlong.

JACK: That's right . . . go on, make a fool of things. Some of us take a
pride in what we do!

PHIL: Ach, pish, Jack! Some of us take a pride in what we do . . . You?
You lot! You're a bunch of no-talent, no-hopers, arse licking your way
up the turkey runner to Barton's office, a fistful of brushes in this

hand and the other one tugging at the forelock . . . "Good morning,
Sir Wallace, by Christ but that's a snazzy Canaletto print up there on
the wall next to that big clock that says a quarter to eight . . .
Suffering Jesus, is that the time already? My, but how time flies when
you're enjoying yourself. Pardon me, while I flick this shite off my
boot . . . Just after stepping on one of Jimmy Robertson's sketches
. . . it'll wash off, I'm sure. What? No, no, not at all, Sir Wallace . . .
of course I don't mind putting in a bit of unpaid overtime . . . it's
results that count, isn't it?" Jack, you wouldn't know a good design
from a plate of Canteen mince. Interest? As soon as Barton starts
revving up his Jag you're the first one out the door and the leg over
the bike before Miss Walkinshaw's even got her teeth out of her
waterjug!

JACK: Yeh . . . yeh . . . very noble . . . very smart. Listen, you ned, I
went to night school for three and a half years . . . I've got a Di-
ploma in Wool Technology!

PHIL: So, what does that mean?

SPANKY: He's haun-knitted.

JACK: One day you're going to go too far, Farrell. When you do . . .
watch out. That's all I'm saying . . . watch out. As for you, McCann
. . . grow up. There's a real world out there. Some of us have to live
in it. *(Exits)*

SPANKY: It's hard to believe he was ever a Slab Boy, isn't it? You don't
suppose there's any truth in the rumour that he's really the love-child
of Miss Walkinshaw and Lon Chaney, Jr? Well, I think I'll stroll
down the Showroom and have a look at the new rugs . . .

PHIL: Eh?

SPANKY: I'm going for a smoke . . . hold the fort. D'you want me to
have a skite for Hector?

PHIL: Christ, I forgot all about him . . .

*(Exit SPANKY)*

*(Pause)*

*(Enter* LUCILLE)

LUCILLE: What've youse been saying to Jack Hogg? He's sitting out there with his face like a half-chewed Penny Dainty.

PHIL: Aw, it's clearing up, is it?

LUCILLE: Bernadette Rooney's boyfriend's going to come up here and give you and your pal a doing if you don't hang off.

PHIL: Hang off what?

LUCILLE: Jack Hogg. They went to school together.

PHIL: Tremble . . . tremble . . .

LUCILLE: It's only Bernadette that's holding him back from coming.

PHIL: Ah, she's a Catholic?

LUCILLE: Eh?

PHIL: Nothing. *(Pause)* Er . . . tell me something, Lucille . . .

LUCILLE: God, is there never any dishes washed in this Slab?

PHIL: See the new guy . . .

LUCILLE: What new guy? Aw . . . him . . . yeh, what about him?

PHIL: Nothing, nothing . . . Just wondered what you thought about him, that's all.

LUCILLE: He's allright. How?

PHIL: Just asking . . .

LUCILLE: What're you asking for?

PHIL: You know he's got scruffula, don't you?

LUCILLE: He's got what?

PHIL: Scruffula. Like very bad impetigo . . . only worse.

LUCILLE: Who told you that rubbish??

PHIL: He caught it off Jack. Tough eh?

LUCILLE: Quit acting it, you.

PHIL: I'm serious. Of course, it's dormant at the moment but any minute his face could just erupt. Him and Jack's been pally for years . . .
Used to live next door to each other . . .

LUCILLE: I never knew that . . .

PHIL: I mean, Jack's as upset about it as everybody else . . . Arthur
included . . .

LUCILLE: I thought his name was Alan?

PHIL: Arthur . . . Alan . . . makes no odds. Another couple of weeks
and nobody's going to recognise him anyhow. Face'll be eaten away
totally . . . just like Jacky Boy's.

LUCILLE: I thought what Jack had wasn't infectious? He told Miss
Walkinshaw he's getting treatment for it . . .

PHIL: He would say that, sweetheart. He's what you call a 'carrier', you
see. Like some people are carriers for infantile paralysis . . . some are
carriers for smallpox . . . Jack's a carrier for plooks. 'Course, you're
okay if you've got 'natural immunity' like I've got . . . look at that
. . . clear as a baby's. *(Shoves his face up next to* LUCILLE*)*

LUCILLE: Gerroff!

PHIL: Not young Aldo, I'm afraid . . . D'you ever see that movie
where the guy gets buried up to his chin in quicksands and they put

this cardboard box full of soldier ants over his noggin and pour treacle through a pin-hole in the top?

LUCILLE: Stop that, you!

PHIL: That's how his features'll be in about three weeks. There's no
known cure for it . . .

LUCILLE: Give us that dish. *(Snatches dish and crosses to sink. Starts
washing it.)*

PHIL: Er . . . Lucille . . .

LUCILLE: What?

PHIL: I was . . . er wondering . . .

LUCILLE: Wondering what? Don't start on about folk with half-eaten-
away faces, I'm warning you.

PHIL: No . . . I was wondering if you'd er . . .

LUCILLE: Wondering if I'd what?

PHIL: If you'd like to . . . er . . .

*(Just then a face appears at the dirty window. It is* HECTOR *half visible
through the dirty glass. He has a bloodstained rag knotted round his
head. He is in his underwear.)*

LUCILLE: Like to what?

PHIL: *(In a rush)* If you'd like to go to the Staffie with me?

LUCILLE: *(Sees face at window)* Aaaaaaaaaaaaaaaaaaaaargh! *(Exits)*

PHIL: What the . . . ? I know I'm not exactly Monty Clift but . . .
*(Sees* HECTOR*)* Godalmighty!!

HECTOR: Let me in, ya bastard! I'm freezing to death out here!

PHIL: *(Throwing window open and dragging* HECTOR *in)* What the hell are you playing at!! We're three floors up!

HECTOR: I climbed up the rone pipe! Ahyah! *(Holds ear)* I've lost a lot of blood from this. Where's my clothes!

PHIL: Making a lovely job of them, son.

HECTOR: Where's my trousers? Are they going to be much longer?

PHIL: No . . . I got Spanky to cut a big daud off them . . . they'll probably come up to about here . . . *(Indicates his kneecap)*

HECTOR: What????

PHIL: Don't be stupid . . . I had a skite at them at dinnertime.

HECTOR: Is it the afternoon already? I must've passed out in the Bobbin Shed . . . ahyah! *(Holds ear)*

PHIL: Shuttup and pull yourself together. Look at the state of you.

HECTOR: That's your fault!! Where's my stuff!!

PHIL: Keep your voice down! I'll go and see if it's ready . . . just quit whining, okay! You stay here . . .

*(Exits only to reappear immediately)*

Willie Curry! . . . Hide!

HECTOR: Waaaaaahhhh!

PHIL: In the cupboard . . . quick!

*(Bundles* HECTOR *into cupboard and stands with his back against the door. Enter* CURRY.)

CURRY: *(Pointing at cupboard)* That's his little hidey-hole, isn't it?

PHIL: Eh?

CURRY: Din't Farrell put it there this morning?

PHIL: Eh?

CURRY: The fresh batch of gum . . . where is it?

PHIL: Er . . . there?

CURRY: *(Turning to look)* Where?

(HECTOR'S *hand appears from cupboard with gumpot.* PHIL *grabs it.)*

PHIL: There.

CURRY: Good God! . . . *(Takes gumpot and moves to door. Stops.)* About this morning, McCann . . .

PHIL: What about this morning?

CURRY: I was only going to say that if you're prepared to pull your socks up . . . toe the line . . . then I'm prepared to forget the whole episode.

PHIL: Yeah?

CURRY: Just show you're willing, McCann . . . that's all I'm asking. These things don't go unnoticed, you know. Mr Barton keeps a weather eye open for lads like yourself . . . ones that buckle down and get on with it. Right? *(Looks at gumpot in hand)* Good God . . . *(Exits)*

PHIL: Thanks, Heck . . .

HECTOR: *(Muffled)* Can I come out now?

PHIL: No . . . you'll only start to annoy me again. I'm not in the mood.

HECTOR: Let me out, ya pig!

PHIL: See what I mean? Shut your face.

HECTOR: What about my clothes!

PHIL: *(Grabbing palette knife)* Shuttit! You're getting your clothes. *(Thrusts knife through edge of door)* One more sound and I swear before the Virgin Mary I'll come in there and slice your beans off!

HECTOR: Ahyah!

*(Exit* PHIL*)*

*(Pause. Enter* SPANKY*)*

SPANKY: I couldn't find the wee fella . . .

HECTOR: *(Muffled, from inside cupboard.)* S'that you, Phil?

SPANKY: *(Looking around)* Eh?

HECTOR: Is the coast clear?

SPANKY: Who is that?

HECTOR: It's me . . . Hector . . .

SPANKY: Aw, yeah *(Looking up)* . . . are you dead?

HECTOR: *(Tumbling out)* Ahyah!

SPANKY: Waaaaaaah! Godalmighty . . . your head!

HECTOR: What's up . . . is it bad!!

SPANKY: No, no . . . it's . . . er . . . s'really stunning.

HECTOR: I had to dive out the lavvy window . . . look at my knees . . . they're all skint.

SPANKY: They go nice with your head.

HECTOR: If Willie catches me like this I'm had it.

SPANKY: You're not forgetting you've to go and see him?

HECTOR: How could I forget? I can't do nothing till my clothes arrive!

SPANKY: Ach, stop your moaning, Heck. You'll just have to be patient.

HECTOR: Patient? Patient?? I'm standing here freezing to death . . . blood running out my ear . . . head nipping with the cold . . . Willie's after me . . . my hands are like two bunches of frozen bananas . . . and you've got the cheek to say be patient!!! Look at my nut! Go on, look! Maybe it is stunning but Christ almight it isn't half gouping! Mammmmmmmy!

SPANKY: *(Alarmed)* Keep your voice down, Hector! And don't keep blaming yourself . . . it was that swine Phil.

HECTOR: And you, ya pig! Where's my clothes????

SPANKY: Shhhhhhhhhh . . . there's somebody coming! Back in your hole, Heck . . . hurry!

*(Bundles* HECTOR *back into cupboard. Enter* JACK HOGG *with* LU-CILLE *at his back.)*

LUCILLE: I'm telling you, Jack . . . I definitely saw something . . . outside the window . . . Mother's life . . . a horrible face, like one of them gargoyles . . . a dirty rag round here and great big staring eyes . . .

JACK: *(Looking out of window)* There certainly doesn't seem to be anything there now, Lucille. You're positive about this 'face'?

LUCILLE: I swear to God. I nearly shit a porcupine. (SPANKY *and* JACK *look at her in disbelief)* Well, I did . . . I got the fright of my life.

JACK: But we're three floors up . . .

LUCILLE: He'll tell you . . . he seen it and all.

SPANKY: Me? I never seen nothing. I've only just came in.

LUCILLE: Were you not here? You were going on about 'soldier ants' and 'treacle' . . .

SPANKY: What is it . . . a recipe?

JACK: Well, there's certainly nothing there now, Lucille . . . so if I could get back to my desk . . . ?

LUCILLE: What? Yeh . . . okay . . . thanks for having a look, Jack . . . but I definitely seen something . . .

JACK: As if I didn't have enough on my plate . . . Women . . . *(Exits) [off.] Gargoyles . . . porcupines . . .*

LUCILLE: Are you absolutely positive?

SPANKY: How could I if I wasn't here?

LUCILLE: Yeh, right enough . . .

SPANKY: Er . . . Lucille . . . while you're here . . .

LUCILLE: *(Preoccupied)* What . . . ?

SPANKY: While you're here I thought I might have a word . . . about the Staffie . . .

LUCILLE: Eh?

SPANKY: The Staff Dance . . . If you fancied . . . you know . . . ?

(HECTOR'S *face appears from the cupboard.* LUCILLE *can see it,* SPANKY *can't.* LUCILLE *screams . . . )*

LUCILLE: Aaaaaaaaaaaaaaargh! *(Exits)*

SPANKY: What was up with her? Honest to God, you ask a civil question . . . *(Sees* HECTOR) Aw, it was you, ya wee shite! You went and gave that doll a helluva fright!

HECTOR: I couldn't help it . . . I was trying to hear what you were saying to her.

SPANKY: I was trying to soften her up for you, ya wee pig!

HECTOR: How was I to know?? I'm sorry . . . Oh, my ear.

*(Enter* PHIL)

PHIL: Ho!

SPANKY: ⎱ Ahyah!!!
HECTOR: ⎰

PHIL: I thought I told you to stay in there? I could've been Willie Curry there.

SPANKY: Not without a series of very painful operations, Phil.

HECTOR: Where's my clothes?? You promised to get my clothes!

PHIL: The doll's putting a hem up on the blouse. (HECTOR *almost has a seizure)* Look, you better make yourself scarce . . . Willie's hovering about like a King Cobra waiting to strike. Give us a hand, Spanks.

HECTOR: Ahyah! Ahyah!

*(They bundle* HECTOR *back into the cupboard)*

*(Enter* ALAN *in brand new white dustcoat.* SPANKY *and* PHIL *start humming 'Dr Kildare' theme. They pick up their palette knives)*

SPANKY: Who's under the knife today, Kildare?

PHIL: It's that young kid that lost both his playpieces in the bus smash, Gillespie.

SPANKY: What group is he, Kildare?

PHIL: Fourteenth Sahara Boy Scouts.

SPANKY: This is gonna be tricky, Doc, there's none in the Frigidaire . . . whadda we gonna do?

PHIL: I'll give him one of my kidneys . . . see if that'll pull him through . . . pore li'l guy.

SPANKY: Is that what was on the pieces?

PHIL: No . . . but I gave my potted heid to the nun we operated on last night.

SPANKY: And how's she doing, Kildare? Did the graft take?

PHIL: I'm afraid not, Doctor . . . it was a Friday. *(Makes a lunge at* ALAN)

ALAN: Hey, watch out! That was a stupid thing to do . . . these things are bloody sharp!

PHIL: Which is more than can be said for you at this precise moment, kiddo. Look at you . . . you're like one of the chorus from 'The Desert Song'! What're you wearing that for?

ALAN: I should've thought that was obvious.

PHIL: Yes, it's certainly that, pal. Don't try sneaking out for a fly smoke unless it's snowing.

*(Enter* CURRY)

CURRY: Fit allright, Alan?

ALAN: Like a glove, Mr Curry.

SPANKY: Is that the thumb hanging out the back?

ALAN: *(Craning round)* Where? (PHIL *snatches his Parker pen)*

CURRY: There's magenta and rose pink needed in the Design Room right away. Jack's on a rush job. McCann . . . Farrell . . . in the cabinet in twenty minutes . . . two large dishes . . . or Mr Barton's going to hear. Okay? Twenty minutes . . . and I don't want to see either of you poking your nose out that door till those shades are ready . . . capeesh? *(Exits)*

SPANKY: Plooky Jack and his plooky rush jobs . . .

PHIL: Better do as he says, Spanks . . . he wasn't kidding. *(Combs his hair)* The young intern'll give you a hand . . .

SPANKY: What about you?

PHIL: I'm waiting on a phonecall.

ALAN: I don't mind helping . . .

SPANKY: No . . . leave it to the pros, kid. You've got something more important to do.

ALAN: Oh?

SPANKY: Yeh . . . pop down to the lavvies and bring up Heck's clobber . . .

ALAN: What?

SPANKY: Togs . . . clothes . . . clobber. Is there something up with you?

ALAN: I don't see that that's more imp . . . (SPANKY *grabs him by the lapels)* Okay, okay . . . I think I can manage . . . *(Exits)*

SPANKY: *(Crossing to cupboard)* Keep breathing, Heck . . . we've sent Snow White for the threads. We'll soon have you out of there . . .

PHIL: And looking a million . . .

SPANKY: Half a million . . . don't exaggerate. Lucille'll be a push-over . . .

PHIL: A cinch . . .

SPANKY: Putty in your hands . . .

PHIL: Don't be dirty, you.

HECTOR: Let me out of here . . . I'm choking!

PHIL: Choke away . . . you're not bothering us, kid.

HECTOR: Help!

PHIL: *(Shoving knife through crack)* What was that?

*(Silence)*

SPANKY: You might've brung his togs up . . .

PHIL: Don't you start. It was difficult enough getting somebody to tackle the bloody things.

SPANKY: Where d'you find the sewing machine?

PHIL: Down the Finishing Department. Promised the doll I'd take her out sometime if she done them for us.

SPANKY: Did she make a nice job of them?

PHIL: Need you ask?

SPANKY: Yeh . . . did she make a nice job of them?

PHIL: I don't know yet, do I? They were wrapped up . . .

SPANKY: She did know what was expected of her?

PHIL: I done a drawing, stupid.

SPANKY: That's alright then. Here . . . d'you want to pulverise some rose pink? *(Dumps a heap of colour onto* PHIL'S *slab)* Heh . . . it wasn't the wee doll with the beerbottle specs you gave the togs to, was it?

PHIL: Look, I'm not really going out with her. I only said that so she'd . . .

*(Enter* ALAN *out of breath and carrying a parcel)*

ALAN: God, that was a close shave . . .

SPANKY: *(Grabbing parcel)* Give us a gander. *(Unwraps parcel and holds trousers up. They look like jodhpurs)* Jeesus . . . who did you draw . . . Lester Piggott?? And look at the shirt! *(Holds shirt up)* What size is Heck??

PHIL: Thirteen and a half.

SPANKY: Not his chest, stupid . . . his neck?

PHIL: Three and five eighths with a muffler on.

SPANKY: Heh, Alfie, you'll need to take these down to the 'Finishing' . . . there's a wee herrie with X-ray goggles . . .

PHIL: Don't be stupid . . . he can hardly find his way to the sink.

SPANKY: Heck's going to look a right palooka in this get-up!

PHIL: Sssssssshhhhh, he'll hear you.

ALAN: How can Hector hear?

HECTOR: *(Stumbling from cupboard)* Hullo?

ALAN: Christ almighty!

PHIL: You'll go to the Bad Fire.

SPANKY: Lookout!!! Somebody's coming!

*(They bundle* HECTOR *back into his cupboard and chuck in his togs behind him. Enter* CURRY.*)*

CURRY: McKenzie still Awol?

SPANKY: You just missed him, Mr Curfew.

CURRY: Where's he hiding himself now, I wonder?

SPANKY: Yeh, that's the question, isn't it?

CURRY: How's that magenta coming along?

SPANKY: *(Grinding furiously)* Aw, not bad . . . just about ready.

CURRY: That's umber, Farrell . . .

SPANKY: Eh?

CURRY: Burnt umber.

SPANKY: S'not my fault . . . I never burnt it!

CURRY: Get some magenta on there toot sweet and no more shenanigans! How's the rose pink, McCann?

(PHIL *dollops a lump on* CURRY'S *hand)*

Still very lumpy! Put some elbow grease into it. You've got another ten minutes or . . . *(Draws finger across throat)* Comprendez? *(Exits)*

PHIL: What is this . . . the bloody Berlitz Academy? Comprendez! Capeeshez . . . cahoochey . . . Capucci . . .

PHIL: ⎫
SPANKY: ⎬ *(Together as they chop and grind at their slabs)*

Comprendez? Capeeshez? Cahoochy? Capucci? Comprendez? Capeeshez? Cahoochy? Capucci? . . .

ALAN: *(Having cleared and dished the burnt umber from* SPANKY'S *slab)* Will I put this out in the cabinet?

(PHIL *and* SPANKY *look at each other)*

PHIL: ⎫ Comprendez?    Capeeshez?
SPANKY: ⎬ Cahoochey? Capucci?

*(Exit* ALAN)

PHIL: Once I get that phonecall . . .

SPANKY: Some mess you made of the boy's napper . . .

PHIL: Eh?

SPANKY: Hector.

PHIL: That's the thanks you get. I spent an hour trying to get him to look like Lucille's dreamboat, Van Johnson . . .

SPANKY: More like Van Gogh the way you went through his ear.

PHIL: S'not easy cutting hair . . . Try it sometime.

*(Re-enter* ALAN)

ALAN: Hey, is it any good . . . ? The Staff Dance . . .

SPANKY: What?

ALAN: The Staffie. Is it good fun?

SPANKY: What you wanting to know for? You're not thinking of buying a ticket, are you?

ALAN: No . . . Curry's just given me his . . . a double. He won't be going. His wife's attending the Foot Clinic . . .

PHIL: That's handy. You don't need to try a leg, do you?

ALAN: I'll probably bump into you there . . .

PHIL: How . . . can you not dance right?

SPANKY: If you fancy a few pints of green wine before you get there let us know . . .

ALAN: I'll think about it . . .

SPANKY: You do that, son . . . so we can tell you where to meet up. *(There is a moaning sound)* What'd you say??

ALAN: I didn't say anything.

*(Another moan . . . )*

SPANKY: Christ . . . Hector!

(HECTOR *promptly falls face first out of the cupboard. He is wearing the restyled clothing.* PHIL *and* SPANKY *rush over . . . )*

PHIL: He's shamming . . . I saw one of his eye-lids flicker.

SPANKY: Wake up, ya wee rat!

ALAN: Give him air, for God's sake . . .

HECTOR: *(Being hauled to his feet)* I think I must've blacked out . . . it got very warm in there . . . Well? What d'you think?

SPANKY: Er . . . s'incredible, Heck . . . just incredible . . . Never seen nothing like it. Right, Phil?

PHIL: That's for sure . . .

HECTOR: *(To* PHIL) What d'you think?

PHIL: Are they comfy? *(He is referring to* HECTOR'S *trousers which he has managed to put on back to front.)*

HECTOR: Yeh. *(Looks down at trouser front)* There's just one thing . . .

PHIL: Ah, you noticed. S'the very latest . . .

HECTOR: Yeh, but how do I go for a . . . ?

PHIL: You don't, son. They run a pipe down your leg into a special ten gallon rubber boot.

ALAN: You've got them on back to front.

SPANKY: Buttons are up the back . . .

PHIL: Just like Uncle Bertie's.

HECTOR: *(Rounding quickly)* What??

PHIL: Just like they had in the Thirties. You must've seen them musicals. Fred Astaire dancing with Roy Rogers. They both had their trousers buttoned up the back . . .

HECTOR: Eh?

PHIL: 'Course you wouldn't've noticed, kid. That's cos Fred wore these long tail coats and Roy . . .

SPANKY: Roy was sitting down . . .

PHIL: On Trigger.

SPANKY: How does the shirt feel? *(Referring to* HECTOR'S *"off-the-shoulder shirt.")*

HECTOR: S'nice and easy on my throat.

SPANKY: Special design . . .

HECTOR: Looks all right then Spanky?

SPANKY: It's a knockout, kid.

PHIL: A knockout.

HECTOR: So you think Lucille'll bite?

PHIL: Your Maw'll be asking you whose the teethmarks are when she give you your bath tonight. Lucille is going to flip.

HECTOR: No kidding, Phil?

ALAN: Hector . . .

(PHIL *holds up Parker pen out of* HECTOR'S *line of vision but so that* ALAN *can see it.)*

HECTOR: D'you like it, Alan?

ALAN: It's . . . er . . . (PHIL *threatens to snap pen)* . . . really gadgey, Heck.

HECTOR: Will I go now and ask her? Will I? *(Heads for door)*

SPANKY: *(Cutting him off)* Not just yet, Hector . . . Remember you've still got to go and see Willie.

HECTOR: Yeh, but I can do that after I've asked Lucille . . .

PHIL: No, Spanky's right, kiddo . . . better go and see Willie first. It's important. Lucille'll not go off the boil. Here, I'll give you my coat to put on . . . *(Takes off coat)*

HECTOR: What do I want that for? I don't mind doing a bit of swanking now that my clothes are up to date.

PHIL: Yeh, but you don't want anybody else to get a preview, do you? Lessen the impact . . . know what I mean? Get the coat on. *(Forces* HECTOR'S *arms into sleeves)*

SPANKY: *(Pulling balaclava helmet from cupboard)* You better put this on and all . . . it's draughty in Willie's room. *(Pulls helmet over* HECTOR'S *head)* Cosy, eh?

HECTOR: *(Slightly bamboozled)* Yeh, but will he not think I'm a bit happed up?

PHIL: That's just it. You've been down at Nurse. Influenza verging on pleurisy. She ordered you home but you decided to soldier on. He'll like that. Maybe not give you your . . . *(Stops)*

SPANKY: *(Quickly)* Wireless back.

HECTOR: I'm not expecting my wireless back. You know what he's like.

SPANKY: Well, you can't expect it back just cos you've got the flu, Heck . . .

PHIL: Triple pneumonia, Spanks.

HECTOR: I'm all mixed up . . . what've I got again?

SPANKY: Triple pneumonia . . .

PHIL: Double rupture . . .

HECTOR: I'll away along then.

SPANKY: Good man. All the best.

PHIL: Good luck, son . . . *(They shove* HECTOR *out the door)* You'll need it.

*(They hold onto each other laughing)*

ALAN: Well, I hope you're proud of yourselves . . . that was a pretty lousy trick to play!

SPANKY: Oh, was it, by jove?

PHIL: A trick, you cad! Take that! *(Bops* ALAN'S *head a smack)*

ALAN: Hey, watch it! That was sore . . . Chuckit! Okay, so I'm speaking out of turn but that poor little bastard's gone off to Willie Curry's office thinking underneath that dustcoat and helmet he really does cut a dash . . . and he'll probably stop off on the way back to have a word with Lucille . . . doff the coat and hat and you know what'll happen then . . . she'll wet herself. Which will probably give you and your crummy friend a big laugh, won't it?

PHIL: Gosh and All Serene . . . the Fifth Form at St Dominic's. Listen, Steerforth Minor, if it wasn't for me and Spanks there that "poor little bastard" wouldn't have any pals. Yeh, that's right. So, we do take the piss . . . set him up a bit . . .

ALAN: More than a bit.

PHIL: Shuttit! Know what he done last Summer?

SPANKY: I don't think he wants to hear, Phil . . .

PHIL: He's talking about us playing dirty tricks? He's going to hear. Know what the mug done? Just cos some stupid lassie wouldn't look the road he was on? Took the string out of his pyjama trousers, tied it round his throat and strung himself up from the kitchen pulley.

SPANKY: His Old Dear had to get the man next door to cut him down with the bread knife. You can still see the rope burns.

PHIL: Touch and go, it was . . .

SPANKY: He still can't swallow a whole chip . . .

PHIL: What me and him's done is give Hector the courage to go and ask Lucille straight out for a date instead of wishing his life away. Okay, so she's going to crease herself but you think twice before you start applying your stupid counterfeit Boys' Own Paper code of 'fair play' in here. You don't know you're living, sweetheart! *(Heads for door. Stops)* And if Willie Curry wants to know where I am, I'm down the bog smoking . . . two fags at once!
*(Exits)*

*(Pause)*

ALAN: Is that true about Hector?

SPANKY: Yeh . . . only I think it was his Old Dear that strung him up from the pulley . . . he can be a right pain at times. How's the rose pink coming along?

ALAN: *(Moves to door)* I'm going to stop him before he makes a complete fool of himself . . .

SPANKY: I wouldn't do that, Alfie . . . you don't know what Phil's like.
(ALAN *hesitates*)
He's got some temper. He once bopped his own jaw for smiling at himself in the mirror. Come on . . . The rose pink's waiting . . .
(ALAN *returns to slab*) Wise boy. Get us they dishes over there . . . the clean ones.

*(Enter JACK HOGG with wages tray)*

JACK: I don't know what I'm doing this for. Lucille should be taking these round. *(Leafs through wage packets)* Farrell . . . G. There you go . . .

SPANKY: Thanks, Jacko. I'll take Phil's and all, he's away to the cludgie.

JACK: McCann . . . McCann . . . Two N's, am I right? McAllister, McBain, McCourtney, McDonald, McFarlane . . . nope, doesn't seem to be anything for him . . .

SPANKY: Stop messing about, Jacky boy.

JACK: There's nothing for him . . . look.

SPANKY: Bloody hell. Give us Hector's then.

JACK: McFarlane, McInnes, McLaughlan, McManus . . . Nothing for Hector either . . . sorry.

SPANKY: Eh?

JACK: There'll be something for you next time, Alan. Won't be a lot, you understand . . . just enough to invest in a gas mask for the occasional sortie into this crap hole. The Boss is trying to fix you up with something a trifle more salubrious for next week. Must dash . . . got a big job on. Oh I've got these mags you wanted to see. Some of your Dad's stuff in one of them. Very nifty. See you.

*(Exits)*

SPANKY: Bloody funny that . . . I was only half surprised at Hector's pay-poke being missing but Phil's and all?

ALAN: Could've been a discrepancy . . .

SPANKY: Eh?

ALAN: An oversight. They might not've put his in with the rest.

SPANKY: Yeh . . . I can see how you got into a University, son. I'll sprint along and have a word with the Cashier. If Phil comes back just say I'm away mending a fuse in Miss Walkinshaw's glass eye . . . okay? *(Exits)*

(ALAN *carries on grinding. Enter* LUCILLE *very warily. She goes to cupboard door and nervously throws it open.)*

ALAN: The gum's over there if you want some.

LUCILLE: No . . . it's not that . . .

ALAN: Oh . . .

LUCILLE: You haven't seen . . . ? *(Opens cupboard. Finds it empty.)*

ALAN: Yes?

LUCILLE: What?

ALAN: You were about to ask if I'd seen something . . .

LUCILLE: Was I?

ALAN: Yes . . . you said, 'You haven't seen . . . ?'

LUCILLE: Oh, yeh, . . . er . . . *(Points to poster of James Dean)* "Rebel Without A Cause" . . . you haven't seen "Rebel Without A Cause" . . . ?

ALAN: That's true. Must've missed it when it came round our way . . .

LUCILLE: What? You've never seen it? Where've you been hiding? *(Offers ALAN some chewing gum)* D'you want a chiclet?

ALAN: Thanks . . . *(Takes a chiclet)*

LUCILLE: Tell us if you think that tastes like ointment. I usually get 'Juicy Fruit' . . . Yeh, it was really brilliant. Me and Bernadette sat through it twice. It was on a double-bill with "East of Eden" . . . Me and her cried our eyes out when his Porsche turned over and he got killed.

ALAN: Ah . . . it was a racing picture?

LUCILLE: What?

ALAN: "East of Eden" . . . it was a racing . . . ?

LUCILLE: I don't find that amusing!

ALAN: Sorry?

LUCILLE: It didn't take you long to get into bad habits, did it!

ALAN: No, you don't understand . . . I wasn't . . .

LUCILLE: Ach, youse are all the same! I hope it's terminal, whatever you got off Jack!

ALAN: Hang on . . . I don't think you . . .

*(Exit* LUCILLE)

Christ, I love Terry Dene. Lucille . . .

*(Enter* PHIL)

PHIL: *(Looking after* LUCILLE) We'll need to get you a cake of Life-buoy, Arthur . . .

*(Enter* SPANKY)

SPANKY: Aw . . . er . . . hi, Phil . . .

ALAN: *(Pointing at poster)* That is whatdyoucallim, isn't it?

PHIL: Miles Malleson . . . ? Yeah. Tragic, eh? There they were . . . Miles . . . Lesley Howard . . . the entire Glen Millar Orchestra . . .

SPANKY: Flying down to Rio . . .

PHIL: When their plane crashed . . .

SPANKY: In the mountains . . .

PHIL: The Urinals . . .

SPANKY: Pilot was pissed.

*(Enter* SADIE *with tea-trolley)*

SADIE: Teas up. There's your dainties . . .

SPANKY:
PHIL:  } Aha!

SADIE: Roobert tarts . . .

SPANKY: Hullo!

SADIE: Chocolate horns . . .

PHIL: Hooray!

SADIE: Penny baps . . .

SPANKY: Whoopee!

SADIE: And your macaroni turnovers . . .

SPANKY:
PHIL:  } Wow!

SADIE: Don't all rush us . . . I know you've just been paid.

PHIL: Hey . . . you never told us the wages was round, Spanks . . . make with the green jobs . . . I'm starving.

SPANKY: I can lend you a couple of bob . . .

PHIL: Quit the kidding . . . I'm ravenous.

ALAN: There wasn't anything for you. Jack Hogg looked twice. Two, please, Sadie, and I'll have one of those . . .

PHIL: What??

SPANKY: That's right, Phil. I've just been along to check with the Cashier. They said you and Heck's was being made up special . . .

PHIL: Suffering Christ . . .

SADIE: Tch, tch, tch, tch . . .
*(To* ALAN) You hold your ears, son.

SPANKY: At least you've got the Art Academy to look forward to. Heck's got sweet damn all . . . absolute piss nothing.

SADIE: Language. Language. That's bloody hellish.

PHIL: What about me? The Art School's still six months away . . .

SADIE: Are you wanting tea, youse two? I'm taking this trolley away in a minute . . .

SPANKY: The lassie'll be phoning soon. It's Hector that's the problem . . . there's only his wages coming into that house. What about his Maw . . . what's he going to tell her?

SADIE: For the last time, are youse two wanting something?

SPANKY: Yeh . . . give us two teas. Want one, Phil?

SADIE: What's up with him?

SPANKY: You want a macaroni cake?

PHIL: You know I've no money, what're you asking us for?

SPANKY: I'll get it. How's about a chocolate horn? You can play 'Old Man River' on it.

PHIL: I'm not wanting nothing!

SADIE: Aw, stick, bubblyjock. *(Pours tea for* SPANKY)

SPANKY: Give us a bap.

SADIE: Thruppence ha'penny.

SPANKY: How come? It's three ha'pence for tea and the baps are a penny.

SADIE: You spent that long making up your mind they've went up. Thruppence ha'penny. (SPANKY *proffers a ten shilling note*) You not got any change? How'm I expected to change a ten shilling note? They're all giving me notes today. Look . . . not a bit of silver in my box. You'll need to get change.

SPANKY: I'll give you it tomorrow, Sadie . . .

SADIE: Tomorrow's Saturday and fine you know it. D'you think I came up the Clyde on this trolley? Get change . . . I'll wait.

SPANKY: You got any, Arthur?

ALAN: I'm not sure . . . *(Takes out Gent's purse)*

PHIL: Christ, where d'you keep that, kid . . . up the leg of your brassiere?

SADIE: I've had enough out of you. One more bit of language and I'll draw my hand across your jaw. Just give that boy there peace . . . what harm has he done you, you bloody . . .

ALAN: No, I don't seem to have that much . . . I can give you a loan of something . . .

SPANKY: No, it's allright . . . I'll do without. *(Bangs bap and tea onto trolley)*

SADIE: You not want these then? The penny bap . . . or the tea?

SPANKY: The tea's cold and the bap's foosty.

SADIE: That's because you're standing there trying to coax Dirty Gub out of his huff . . .

PHIL: Aw, piss off, you old trollop.

SADIE: I heard that . . . I heard that, ya hooligan! *(Smacks* PHIL *on head)* If one of my boys was here he'd stoat you off that wall, so he would.

PHIL: Ahyah! Ohyah! *(Clutches head)* You hit us with your ring! Owwww.

SADIE: Aye, you're the big cheese in here, Philip McCann, but just you wait . . . somebody's going to sort you out before you're much older. Talk to me like that, would you! Just you wait . . . (ALAN *holds door open)* Thanks, son . . . you're a gentleman.

PHIL: Ow . . . that was some skelp . . .

SPANKY: Here . . . put that on it. *(Hands* PHIL *an éclair that he's pinched)*

PHIL: Ta . . . What'd she go and hit us for?

SPANKY: She's at a funny age. My Maw's the same . . . lashes out at the bree and me for nothing. The Sunday Post Doctor says it's nothing to worry about . . . they all go like that. These are good aren't they?

ALAN: That is Terry Dene, isn't it?

SPANKY: Where? *(Looks inside éclair)*

ALAN: Come on . . . is it . . . Terry Dene?

SPANKY: You ignorant or something?

ALAN: The one that was in "Rebel Without A Cause" and "East of Aden" . . . ?

SPANKY: Suez . . . "East of Suez".

ALAN: About motor racing . . . ?

SPANKY: That's the one . . . only it was camels. Him and Frankie Laine raced round the Sphinx for Audrey Murphy's hand. Frankie won by a nose so they gave him Audrey's hand. Terry got the rest of her . . . right?

PHIL: Think I'll take a walk, Spanks . . .

SPANKY: You not want to hang about in case that phonecall comes?

PHIL: No . . . don't think I'm going to hear anyhow . . . it's that kind of day. If the doll phones you take it . . . say you're me . . . okay?

SPANKY: Okay . . . if you're sure.

*(Exit PHIL)*

ALAN: That's the rest of the pink dished . . . will I put it out in the cabinet . . . ?

SPANKY: No . . . put it out in the cabinet.

*(Exit ALAN. Pause. Enter JACK HOGG)*

JACK: I'm looking for your chum.

SPANKY: What're you wanting him for?

JACK: There's a phonecall in Mr Barton's office . . . sounded rather urgent. Girl said it was the hospital.

SPANKY: That's all right, I'll take it.

JACK: No, no . . . she was most insistent she speak to McCann himself . . .

SPANKY: I'll take it, I said . . .

JACK: No, I don't think . . .

SPANKY: I'm authorised! *(Exits)*

JACK: Hey . . . *(Exits)*

*(Pause. Enter* SADIE)

SADIE: Too bloody soft, that's my trouble . . . He's not getting off with it, this time. Fifteen shillings? Not on your nelly . . . *(Sits down. Eases shoes off)* Oooooohhhhh . . . I should trade these in for a set of casters . . .

*(Enter* LUCILLE. *Crosses to sink)*

Any Epsom salts, hen?

LUCILLE: Waaahh! God, it's you! What're you playing at, Sadie!

SADIE: Have you seen that shy boy McCann on your travels?

LUCILLE: Shy?

SADIE: Aye . . . fifteen bob shy. He still owes us for that Dance ticket he got.

LUCILLE: Not again? When're you going to wise up? You'll just need to wait and grab him at the Town Hall . . .

SADIE: Oh, no . . . I'll not be seeing any Town Hall the night, sweetheart. If I thought these had to burl me round a dance floor . . . *(Cradles feet)*

LUCILLE: Are you not going? Aw, Sadie, it was a right scream last year.

SADIE: I know, flower . . .

LUCILLE: That man of yours was a howl.

SADIE: Aye . . . hysterical. Who else would sprint the length of the hall with a pint of Younger's in their fist and try leapfrogging over the top of Miss Walkinshaw with that beehive hairdo of hers . . . eh? Only that stupid scunner I've got . . .

LUCILLE: How long was he off his work with the leg?

SADIE: Too long, sweetheart. He had my heart roasted, so he did. Sitting there with the bloody leg up on the fender shouting at me to put his line on at the bookie's for him. "See that?" I says . . . "If you're not up and back to your work tomorrow I'll draw this across your back!" I had the poker in my hand . . . and I would've done it and all. Had me up to high doh. Couldn't get the stookie down the dungarees quick enough. Men? I wouldn't waste my time, hen.

LUCILLE: Come off it, Sadie . . .

SADIE: I'd to take the first one that came along. I'd've been better off with a lucky bag.

LUCILLE: They're not all like that, for God's sake.

SADIE: You'll learn, flower . . . you're young yet. You can afford to sift through the dross . . . till you come to the real rubbish at the bottom.

LUCILLE: Not this cookie. Lucille Bentley . . . Woman of the World . . . Fling Out Your Men!

SADIE: Wait till you get to my age and all you've got to show's bad feet and a display cabinet . . .

LUCILLE: Who wants to get to your age?

SADIE: Here, what time is it? I promised 'Leapfrog' I'd get him a nice bit of fish for his tea. Well, it's Friday . . . with any luck he'll be home with half his paypoke still on him . . .

LUCILLE: Yeh, and it'll be his own half, by the sounds of it. You wouldn't get me putting up with that.

SADIE: I'm biding my time, sweetheart. Soon as I've a good wee bankbook I'm showing that swine the door. See that? *(Indicates breast)* I lost that over the head of him.

LUCILLE: My God, what did he do??

SADIE: Flang it in the midden.

LUCILLE: Eh?

SADIE: Thought it was one of our James's old footballs that got bursted.

LUCILLE: What?

SADIE: No, no . . . I had that off long before I got in tow with that sod. Up the Western . . .

*(Enter* SPANKY. *He is preoccupied.)*

Hey, you, where's your pal?

SPANKY: Eh?

SADIE: Fifteen bob for a dance ticket I'm after . . .

SPANKY: Aw, yeh . . . *(Reaches in pocket for money)*

SADIE: Mr Anderson . . . big strapping man . . . head surgeon up there . . . *(Taking money from* SPANKY*)* Thanks, son. *(To* LUCILLE*)* "That'll have to come away, Miss Jowett, otherwise it'll go right through your whole system. Six months and you'll be a goner." *(To* LUCILLE*)* Couldn't argue with that, flower.

SPANKY: Hey . . . *(Checks money)*

SADIE: Felt a bit lopsided at first but I kept my trolley money in this pocket till I got my balance back.

SPANKY: Hey, Sadie . . .

SADIE: They've went away up as well. Nineteen and eleven for a replacement.

LUCILLE: *(To* SPANKY) I hope you and your pal catch it off Jack and all . . .

SPANKY: Eh?

*(Exit* LUCILLE)

SADIE: Nineteen and eleven . . . for a single . . .

SPANKY: Used to be only fifteen bob . . .

SADIE: Aye, but they're made of foam rubber now, son. *(Exits)*

SPANKY: Eh? Hey, Sadie . . . *(Crosses to door)*

*(Enter* PHIL *at the gallop)*

PHIL: Well?

SPANKY: What way did the old bag go?

PHIL: You took a phonecall . . . Jack says . . .

SPANKY: Oh, yeh . . . from the . . . er . . . hospital . . .

PHIL: And?

SPANKY: The doll thought I was you. You told me to say I was you . . .

PHIL: I know that! Hurry up!

SPANKY: It was the hospital.

PHIL: I know! Tell us the worst.

SPANKY: Your Maw's vanished.

PHIL: What??

SPANKY: Shot the crow . . . skedaddled.

PHIL: You mean it really was the hospital?

SPANKY: That's what I was trying to tell you, Phil . . .

PHIL: Christ.

SPANKY: They were phoning to see if she'd been in touch with me . . . you, I mean. They said not to be alarmed . . .

PHIL: Not to be alarmed?? What if she turns up here? She'll probably put a hatchet through old Walkinshaw's head just to give me a showing up.

*(Enter* ALAN*)*

SPANKY: They've sent some people out to look for her.

PHIL: She can be real vicious, you know. She once took a bite out of a guy's nose up at the Out Patients . . .

SPANKY: Eh?

PHIL: It was only the Occupational Therapist. Jeeesus Christ, how come I couldn't have a sensible Maw like you guys . . . eh?

SPANKY: You don't know that our Maws is any more sensibler than yours, Phil . . .

PHIL: All my stupid Maw ever done was worry. Worry about money . . . about schools . . . going to Mass . . . missing confessions . . . going out with lassies . . . getting our hole. Some bloody hope! All we ever knew about dames was their arms stuck out sideyways when they ran.

SPANKY: Most of our Maws is a bit like that . . .

PHIL: I bet you his isn't!

SPANKY: Leave him alone, Phil . . . he doesn't know what you're talking about.

PHIL: I bet you he doesn't. *(To* ALAN) What do you know about getting up in the middle of the night in your shirt tail to say five decades of the rosary over your Maw's open wrists? What do you know about screaming fits and your old man's nut getting bopped off the Pope's calendar? What do you know about razor blades and public wards and row upon row of gumsy cadavers all sitting up watching you stumble in with your Lucozade and excuses? Christ, what one's mine? Is that you, Maw? What do you know about living in a rabbit hutch with concrete floors and your Old Man's never in and you're left trying to have a conversation with a TV set and a Maw that thinks you're St Thomas Aquinas? What do you know about standing there day in, day out in the Factor's office asking for a move and the guy with the shiny arse on his trousers shakes his head and treats your Old Dear like dirt??

ALAN: All right . . . you've had your say but I don't see where I come in . . .

PHIL: Well, it certainly isn't the 'Tradesman's Entrance', petal. Straight up to the front door for you . . . "This way, sir. Let me take your problems, sir . . . they must be cutting into your shoulder". I know where I'd like to cut into you! *(Makes a lunge at* ALAN)

SPANKY: *(Intervening)* Steady on, Phil! I don't think Archie's any idea what . . .

PHIL: That's right, Spanky old sport, you stick with his lot. You always did know what side your madeira cake was buttered!

SPANKY: That's not fair. I was only . . .

PHIL: I'm away to join the Hunt. I'll send my Maw's head back for your Dad's Trophy Room . . . Alan! *(Using his right name for the first time with derisive emphasis.)*

SPANKY: What about your wages?

PHIL: Stuff them up Curry's jaxie . . . I'm off. *(Exits)*

*(Off)* Tally-hoooooooooooooooo . . .

*(Pause)*

SPANKY: You don't want to pay too much attention to Phil, son . . . he reads a lot.

ALAN: I think he's off his chump. *(Pause)* Was that true, all that . . . ? About his mother trying to . . . you know . . . ?

SPANKY: Do away with herself? S'true all right. Last time it happened was at a boarding house in Dunoon. His Old Man found the suicide note tucked into her beach bag. She'd went and swallowed a hundred and fifty aspirins . . . washed down with a bottle of Domestos . . .

ALAN: I thought he mentioned razor blades . . . ?

SPANKY: C'mon, Arthur . . . she'd need to be a real looney to swallow a hundred and fifty razor blades . . . No . . . they made her be sick down the toilet . . . phoned for the ambulance. Landlady was quite sympathetic . . . till Phil's Maw brung up the bleach and took the flowers off her wallpaper. Did you say the rest of the rose pink was ready?

ALAN: It's in the cabinet . . .

SPANKY: Here . . . you can have a 'nice time' with the Hooker's green, honey . . .

*(Enter JACK HOGG)*

JACK: That's McCann's wages. Has he got a bonus or what? Right hefty wage packet. Hector not about? I've got his too. God, feel the weight of that. Have they been putting in a bit of overtime?

SPANKY: I'll take that, Jacky Boy. *(Takes PHIL's wage packet)*

JACK: Would you see that Heck gets that one, Alan? I think we can trust you.

SPANKY: And what's that supposed to mean, Plooky Appearance?

JACK: Why don't you dry up?

SPANKY: Like you, Jacky Boy? Not bloody likely. You know you can get stuff for that? You rub it all over your phissog. It's cried emery paper.

JACK: Ho . . . bloody, ho. Look what's talking. Look at the arms. It's like somebody's put a dustcoat on a chimp.

SPANKY: There's nothing up with my arms!

JACK: They're about seven inches longer than your legs.

SPANKY: Three and half . . . don't exaggerate!

*(Enter* PHIL*)*

I thought you were away?

PHIL: I went along for my wages . . . doll said she gave them to Jack.

JACK: The monkey's got them . . .

SPANKY: Catch. *(Flings packet to* PHIL*)* S'that you off, Jackknife? Not fancy a hot poultice before you go?

JACK: If you need a lift home, Alan, let me know . . . I'll try and arrange something . . .

ALAN: Thanks.

*(Exit* JACK*)*

SPANKY: *(To* PHIL *who is opening his wage packet)* Your books?

PHIL: Yeh . . . P45, the lot . . . *(Reads document)* "Non Contributory Pension Scheme" . . . what's that?

ALAN: It means you haven't paid directly into . . .

PHIL: Shuttit, you! I'm talking to my friend. Well?

SPANKY: How should I know? I've got all these dishes to wash. Can you not give us a hand? There's hundreds of them.

PHIL: You're forgetting something, Spanky. I don't work here any more.

SPANKY: You never did, Phil.

PHIL: Less of the sarcasm . . . *(sarcastically)* Slab Boy.

SPANKY: At least I still am one.

PHIL: Yeh . . . how come? Me and Hector get the heave and you're still here washing dishes safe and secure. How d'you manage it, eh?

SPANKY: Going to get out of my road? I've got work to do . . .

PHIL: Work? Has Noddy there been getting to you?

SPANKY: Why don't you can it, Phil? Me and the boy wants to get cleared up.

PHIL: Aw . . . it's "me and the boy" now, is it?

SPANKY: Yeh . . . what of it?

PHIL: I think I'm going to be sick.

SPANKY: Well, don't hang over the shades, there's gum in them al- . . .

(PHIL *grabs him. They confront one another)*

*(Enter* CURRY)

CURRY: Still here, McCann? You can go any time, you know.

PHIL: I'm waiting for a phonecall.

CURRY: Only urgent personal calls allowed . . .

PHIL: This is urgent. I'm waiting for word from the hospital.

CURRY: What's up . . . someone in the family ill?

PHIL: It's my Maw.

CURRY: Oh, yes, of course. Were the lacerations severe? It can do a great deal of damage, plate glass . . .

PHIL: What?

CURRY: Plate glass . . . the stuff they have in shop windows.

PHIL: What d'you know about shop windows? Who told you about it?

CURRY: There was a bit in today's Paisley Express . . . "Ferguslie Park Woman In Store Window Accident" . . .

PHIL: It wasn't an accident. She meant to do it.

CURRY: Eh? But the paper said your mother was thrown through the window by a passing car . . .

PHIL: Well, they got it wrong, didn't they? There was a car there but it wasn't passing . . . it was parked. What she done was take a header off the roof . . . straight through the Co window . . . simple.

CURRY: From the roof of a car? She must've been badly injured.

PHIL: Not a scratch. They say it was the angle she jumped off the roof of the motor.

CURRY: Good God, it must've been a miracle.

PHIL: Nope . . . a Ford Prefect.

CURRY: You're a callow bastard, McCann. As soon as that phonecall comes through you can sling your hook . . . okay! Alan . . . my office.
*(Exeunt CURRY and ALAN)*

SPANKY: I say, Nugent, d'you think I should've leapt into the scrum just then and chinned old Quelch about getting into Upper School? Hmmm?

PHIL: Yes, you might've been lucky and got the bag like me, old chap.

SPANKY: Some hope . . . I'm here for the duration.

PHIL: Well, if you play your cards right . . . don't give the screws too much cheek . . . time off for good behaviour . . . who knows, you might get it down to "life".

SPANKY: What about Pygmy Minimus? He thought he was here for life.

PHIL: So?

SPANKY: D'you not think we should put round the hat? Help tide him over till he gets his Broo money?

PHIL: What about tiding me over till I get mine?

SPANKY: You've got the Art College to look forward to.

PHIL: And my nearest and dearest wandering the fields and hedgerows eating worms.

SPANKY: C'mon, what d'you say? Just to see the boy's Mammy over the hump . . .

PHIL: *(Looking in wage packet)* Over the hump? There's hardly enough in here to buy Quasimodo a half of Bell's.

SPANKY: Ten bob'll do . . . look, I'll match it.

PHIL: Make it five. Don't say I'm not generous . . .

SPANKY: Ten. Come on . . .

PHIL: *(Hands over ten shilling note)* Stupid, but not ungenerous.

SPANKY: Heck'll not forget this, Phil.

PHIL: Nor will I . . . that's half my bloody wages.

SPANKY: May the sausage of true contentment sizzle in your sandwich.

PHIL: Confucius?

SPANKY: Tex Ritter . . . he sang it in a movie once. Right, I'll get this in an envelope, will I?

PHIL: Not be better with an armour-plated truck?

SPANKY: Let's have a celebration. Here's two bob . . . race down the canteen and bring us back a thousand Woodbine.

PHIL: Terrific. Open, Sesame.

SPANKY: Voila.

PHIL: Back'n a tricycle. *(Exits)*

SPANKY: *(Writing on wage packet containing* HECTOR'S *"presentation")* Hector "Threads" McKenzie . . . Slab Boy . . . Retired. Farewell, small chum . . . it has been fun, but now your days are numbered . . . We've had our laughs . . . we've shared our tears . . . You've left me effing lumbered.

*(Enter* LUCILLE. *She crosses to sink)*

SPANKY: Hi Lucille. Replenishing the old 'jooga di aqua', I see.

LUCILLE: You trying to be filthy again?

SPANKY: It's Italian . . .

LUCILLE: Where'd you get it . . . off a chip poke?

SPANKY: D'you hear about Hector?

LUCILLE: Hear what?

SPANKY: He's going to be leaving us . . .

LUCILLE: Am I supposed to pass out or something? You should all be leaving. You're a bunch of good-for-nothing foul mouthed pigs . . . in a foul-smelling pig sty. Take a look at this joint . . . what d'you see?

SPANKY: We're waiting for the decorators . . .

LUCILLE: It's an absolute cowp. You're frightened to come in here in case you get something contagious. And by the way that isn't true what you said about the new guy . . . I checked with Jack. What Jack's got is described as 'Parched Skin' . . . and it is not smittal, so there.

SPANKY: Ah . . . that's good news.

LUCILLE: You're a bunch of lying dogs. And you're bone idle . . . look at all them manky dishes.

SPANKY: Let lying dogs sleep, I always say. Er . . . Lucille, I was wondering . . .

LUCILLE: Here we go again. Yes?

SPANKY: I was wondering if you . . . er . . . caught my drift earlier on?

LUCILLE: And what drift was that?

SPANKY: The Staffie . . . ?

LUCILLE: The Staffie?

SPANKY: Staff Dance . . .

LUCILLE: Aw . . . that's what you call it? How childish.

SPANKY: If you fancied going with . . . ?

LUCILLE: Fancied going with who? Not you?

SPANKY: Yeah . . . what's up with me? I know you aren't booked . . .

LUCILLE: Oh, do you?

SPANKY: I checked with Miss Walkinshaw. How about it, eh? I'm getting a gadgey dinner suit from "Caled . . ." from "Jackson's" . . . real honey . . . roll collar . . . swivel button . . . fingertip drape . . . Yeh, I know my arms look a bit on the long side but the guy in the shop said that was no problem . . . he's going to break them off at the elbows for us. What d'you say? Eh? What're you staring at?

LUCILLE: I can't believe the cheek of you guys. Have you looked in a mirror lately?

SPANKY: 'Course I have . . . every morning when I'm shaving. I've got a very heavy growth, you know. Feel.

LUCILLE: Don't come near me.

SPANKY: C'mon, cut the capers, Lucille . . . are you going to the Dance or are you not going to the Dance?

LUCILLE: Oh, I'm going okay . . .

SPANKY: Terrific. What time d'you want me to . . . ?

LUCILLE: But not with you, sonny boy. I'm booked.

SPANKY: What? Who're you going with? I never heard nothing.

LUCILLE: That's because your listeners are run up from the same material as your rompers . . . shoddy flannelette.

SPANKY: C'mon, who is it? Who are you going with?

LUCILLE: Excuse me . . .

SPANKY: Don't be lousy . . . tell me who it is.

LUCILLE: All I'm saying is . . .

SPANKY: Yeh?

LUCILLE: . . . It's someone from the Slab Room. Now, shift.

SPANKY: Eh?

LUCILLE: Shift, I said. Move the torso.

SPANKY: Sure . . .

*(Enter* PHIL*)*

PHIL: Ah . . . Lucille . . . help yourself to a cork-tipped Woodbine . . . Don't scar the chest, throat or lungs . . . just tear the skin off your lips. On you go, I've got hundreds . . .

(JACK HOGG *looks round the door*)

JACK: Farrell . . . Boss wants to see you. I mean now.

PHIL: Oho. Put this behind your ear, kiddo. *(Places Woodbine behind* SPANKY'S *ear)* When he offers you the desk . . . light up . . . that'll impress him.

SPANKY: Thanks . . .

JACK: And you better quit spreading lies, McCann. This is non-transmittable. Serious but non-transmittable. Right, Farrell, follow me . . .
*(Exeunt)*

LUCILLE: Let me out as well . . .

PHIL: Hold your horses, sweetheart.

LUCILLE: Let me past, I said.

PHIL: Wait a second . . . this is important.

LUCILLE: Aw, yeh? What is it? I'm dying to know . . .

PHIL: *(stifles yawn)*. You're going to the Dance tonight, right?

LUCILLE: If this is a mind-reading act it's pathetic.

PHIL: I know it's asking a lot but . . . you don't have a date . . . right? *(Pause)* Have you or have you not got a date?

LUCILLE: I might have . . .

PHIL: When did this happen?

LUCILLE: Couple of minutes ago . . .

PHIL: Bloody hell. You can break it, can't you? C'mon, doll, you can break it.

LUCILLE: All right . . . yeh . . . maybe. Depends who asks.

PHIL: I'm asking.

LUCILLE: Then I'll think about it . . .

PHIL: Yes or no?

LUCILLE: Quit pressing me . . . I said I'd think about it . . . okay, yeh.

PHIL: Terrific. You're a doll.

LUCILLE: What time are you picking us up at?

PHIL: No, no . . . you don't understand, sweetheart. Not me . . . Hector.

LUCILLE: What!

PHIL: Look, I know me and Spanks take the piss out of him but underneath he's . . .

LUCILLE: This is another one of your jokes, isn't it!

PHIL: 'Course it isn't . . . I'm dead serious. What would I want to . . .

LUCILLE: Hector! I'd rather play Postman's Knock with Jack Hogg!

PHIL: You don't have to dance every dance with the wee shite . . . just come in the door with him . . .

LUCILLE: Not on your life! Move!

PHIL: He's crazy about you, for Christ's sake!

LUCILLE: So what!!

PHIL: It's all he ever thinks about . . . the Big Date . . . the Staffie . . . The guy's in love with you, Lucille.

LUCILLE: Don't talk romantic. I wouldn't be seen dead with that smout at a dance. You're off your head, Phil McCann. I'd be laughed out of the Design Room.

PHIL: Listen . . . you only have to give the boy the impression you're with him . . . flash him the occasional smile . . . the odd nibble at his ear . . . not this one . . . me and Spanks'll do the rest . . . get him that pissed he'll never notice you're not around for the rest of the night . . .

LUCILLE: Thanks a bunch.

PHIL: You know what I mean. As long as he thinks you've went with him.

LUCILLE: No, I said . . . what do I have to do? Carve it in letters this size on my forehead? N-O! I've never heard anything so ridiculous. He's a dwarf, for God's sake!

PHIL: Even dwarves have feelings, doll. Christ, don't you have any? Where's your compassion . . . your sensitivity . . . your eye to the main chance? Alexander Pope was a dwarf . . . so was Lautrec . . . so was Turner . . . and what were they? Giants. That's what they were . . . giants. Jesus God Almighty . . . he's nuts about you . . . can't you see that?

LUCILLE: He's a mess! Get out of my road! Get out of my life!

PHIL: Lucille . . .

*(Exit* LUCILLE)

Aaaaaaahhhh . . . fuck it!

*(Pause. Enter* SPANKY)

What'd Barton want? *(Silence)* You don't have to spare my feelings, kiddo . . . I'm off to pastures new. Where's your desk to be . . . next to Jimmy Robertson's? *(Silence)* Miss Walkinshaw's *(Silence)* Aw, no . . . not beside Jack Hogg?

SPANKY: He told us to wire in and I just might get one in about eighteen months time . . .

PHIL: Jeesus . . . I hope you told him where to stick it?

SPANKY: Not in so many words, no. *(Pause)* You been talking to Lucille?

PHIL: Eh? What's it to you?

SPANKY: About the Dance? Yeh, she said . . . *(Pause)* Give us one of them Woodies, will you?

PHIL: You can have the lot. They keep them stacked up beside the kippers down there.

*(They light up. Enter* HECTOR*)*

HECTOR: I've seen him . . .

SPANKY: Seen who? Bela Lagoosey? You're as white as a sheet . . .

HECTOR: Willie . . . I've just came from his office . . .

SPANKY: Get the boy a seat, Phil . . . *(They sit* HECTOR *down)*

HECTOR: I had to be sick down the toilet . . .

SPANKY: So you know then?

HECTOR: Yeh . . . I know. I came back to clear out my stuff. What's that funny smell?

PHIL: Fishbine. D'you want a drag? It'll clean out what's left in your stomach, kid.

SPANKY: Heh . . . the Presentation, Phil . . .

PHIL: I don't think I'm up to it, Spanks . . .

SPANKY: Nor me . . . we'll just have to force ourselves . . . look at the pale he is . . .

PHIL: Still in a state of shock, the boy . . .

SPANKY: Er . . . Hecky . . .

HECTOR: *(Getting up weakly)* Any of you guys seen my sables?

SPANKY: We'd like to present this little . . . er . . . this token of . . . er . . .

HECTOR: There was five of them . . . plus a squared-off fitch with my name on it . . .

SPANKY: Are you going to shut your face and listen, Shorty? Me and Phil's trying to make a Presentation here . . .

PHIL: It's a quid.

SPANKY: Shuttup.

HECTOR: Sorry, what were you saying?

SPANKY: We know it's come as a bit of a surprise to you, Hector . . . you having to leave the Slab Room . . .

HECTOR: It's a bombshell . . . no kidding . . .

SPANKY: *(To* PHIL*)* Doesn't make it easy, does he? Er . . . so what me and Phil's done is . . . er . . . well, we put round the hat and . . . er . . .

PHIL: Carry on, you're doing fine.

SPANKY: . . . It's not a lot, you understand . . .

PHIL: It's a quid, son.

SPANKY: Shuttup, will you!

PHIL: Give us it. *(Snatches 'presentation')* What Spanky was trying to say, Hector, is . . . er . . . och, here.

SPANKY: It's a quid.

*(They clap)*

HECTOR: What's this for?

PHIL: Not even a "Thank you, boys, I'm really touched". You are leaving the Slab Room, right?

HECTOR: Yeh, but . . .

SPANKY: Then that'll tide you over . . . you and your Maw . . .

PHIL: Till you get another job.

HECTOR: Eh?

SPANKY: He said, till you get another job.

HECTOR: Eh?

SPANKY: } Till you get another job!
PHIL: }

HECTOR: I've already got another job.

PHIL: Christ, that was quick. Is there a mobile Broo outside?

HECTOR: That's what I was along seeing Willie about . . . my new job . . . I start on a desk on Monday.

SPANKY: } *(Together)* What????
PHIL: }

HECTOR: I'm a designer now. Seven quid a week backdated a fortnight, rising in annual increments to twelve pounds, fifteen and eleven after tax at the end of four years. God, I don't think I feel too well . . .

SPANKY: Me too . . .

HECTOR: It's the excitement.

*(Enter* ALAN*)*

ALAN: Hey . . . guess what? Since two of you guys are vacating the Slab, Curry thought I should step in and fill the breach . . . how about that? Where are the gum crystals kept again? *(Hunts around)* Oh . . . there was a phonecall came through to Willie's office . . . I said I'd pass the message on . . .

PHIL: Eh? Is my Maw safe??

ALAN: You didn't get in.

PHIL: What?

ALAN: Exceptionally high number of applicants this year . . . something like that . . .

PHIL: Christ . . .

ALAN: Hey . . . well done, Heck . . . Jack's just told me . . .

*(Enter* LUCILLE *dressed for home)*

LUCILLE: Burton's Corner . . . quarter to . . . okay?

(PHIL *and* SPANKY *look towards each other)*

ALAN: Yeh . . . right, Lucille.

PHIL: ⎱
SPANKY: ⎰ *(Together) Eh??*

LUCILLE: Are you sure you can get your Dad's M.G.?

ALAN: No problem . . .

LUCILLE: And put some cream on that pimple . . . I swear it's twice the size it was this morning.

ALAN: For God's sake . . .

LUCILLE: *(To* PHIL) Sorry . . . I couldn't've went through with it even if I had said, yeh . . . you can see that, can't you? I mean to say . . . look at him . . . he's a skelf.

PHIL: You're looking at a skelf that's branching out, doll . . .

LUCILLE: Aw, go to hell. And if I was you I wouldn't go home via Storey Street . . . that's where Bernadette's boyfriend's got his jew-jipsey parlour. He eats smouts like you for his breakfast! *(To* ALAN) If you're not there on the dot I'm going in by myself so be warned! *(Exits)*

ALAN: Listen, Heck . . .

HECTOR: *(Bravely)* Don't worry about it, Alan . . . I'm taking Willie Curry on my ticket. Well, you guys, I better shoot off . . . Willie's giving us a lift down the road. You can keep that fitch if you find it, anybody.

*(Changes into overcoat)*

SPANKY: Heh . . . hold on, Hector . . . you can't go just like that. What about that money we gave you?

HECTOR: Aw, yeh . . . a quid, wasn't it? No . . . I'll just hold onto that, if youse don't mind. Help towards a skin graft for my ear and the down payment on a nylon overall like Jimmy Robertson's got. 'Night all . . . *(Exits)*

SPANKY: The cocky little . . .

(HECTOR *re-enters)*

HECTOR: And I'll be expecting some smart grinding from this department in the future. No palming me off with substandard shades, Farrell. Oh . . . sorry to hear you lost your job, Phil. Not to worry . . . you'll not find much difference now you're "officially" out of work.

*(Takes Parker pen from* PHIL'S *pocket and hands it to* ALAN) See youse at the Staffie. *(Exits)*

ALAN: I better push off, too . . . heavy night ahead. *(Changes for home)*

SPANKY: Christ, I even let him into the secrets of gum making . . .
what happens? He strolls off into the sunset with the dame hanging
from his top lip. Yeh, I think you better push off, Archie . . . go on
. . . beat it.

(ALAN *crosses to door . . . stops*)

ALAN: *(To* PHIL) There's always next year, you know . . .

PHIL: You heard . . . beat it!

ALAN: Fine. I was going to say 'sorry' but I can see you're doing a
pretty good job of that on your own. See you at the Dance . . . buy
you a small beer, perhaps? And I'll be seeing you on Monday . . .
Sparky . . . so take it easy on the floor . . . watch out nobody steps
on your fingers . . . there's quite a bit of grinding to get through . . .
That cabinet out there's an embarrassment . . .

(PHIL *and* SPANKY *pick up missiles. Exit* ALAN *very smartly. The door
gets the brunt of it*)

(*Enter* JACK HOGG *with note*)

JACK: Alan not around? Tch . . . he never said whether he was going
on this trainspotters outing on Sunday . . . This was left at the Gate-
house for you, McCann. Ambulancemen said to give it to you
straight away. I don't know what I'm delivering bloody messages for
. . . I'm supposed to be on a Top Priority rush job. Cheer up, Farrell,
you'll feel at home once you're in your monkey suit tonight . . .
owwwww! *(Exits)*

SPANKY: One of these days I'm really going to knock spots off that guy.
*(Pause)* Your Maw?

PHIL: *(Reads)* "Got your Mum in the back of the wagon. The boys in
blue managed to fish her out of the river without too much difficulty.
The grappling hooks did not break the skin. Regards to your Dad
and tell him Sammy Cairns will see him at Shawfield tonight as usual.
'Loopy Looloo', Trap Five, is a cert, tell him. All the best. S. Cairns.
Driver. St Andrew's Ambulance Service".

SPANKY: At least you know she's back in captivity . . . in safe hands, I mean. You can go to the Staffie and enjoy yourself now . . .

PHIL: Yeh . . .

SPANKY: Wonder what she was doing in the river?

PHIL: Water therapy. *(Screws up note and pops it in gumpot)*

*(Enter* CURRY *dressed for going home.)*

CURRY: Hector not here? Expect he's waiting at the car. Here, is there enough gum for Jack? *(Picks up gumpot)* I'll take this out to him . . . Wait a mo . . . there's a foreign body in here . . .

PHIL: What is it . . . a Jap?

CURRY: *(Pouring contents out)* You'll just have to make up some fresh stuff, Farrell . . . Mr Barton's waiting on that job Jack's doing so . . .

SPANKY: I'm getting ready to go home, Mr Curry . . . it's the Staffie tonight.

CURRY: Never you mind about that . . . the Staff Dance can wait . . . Mr Barton can't. Get that overall back on and get weaving. And you can give him a hand, McCann . . . the muslin's down there. Come on, look alert. I often wonder how a pair of greasy-quiffed nancy boys like you would've fared in the tropics. By God, you had to be on your toes out there . . . Slant-eyed snipers up every second palm tree, drawing a bead on us jocks as we cut and hacked a path through the dense undergrowth. Is this what Wingate gave up his last gasp for? So that louts like you could get yourselves a cushy little number? Get into those crystals.

PHIL: *(Stops what he's doing)* Hey . . . wait a minute. What am I doing here? Wingate . . . snipers . . . ? You're forgetting something, Curry . . . I don't work here any more, remember? And while we're at it, you can drop all that gibbon-shit about the jungle. Jimmy Robertson blew the gaff. The only stuff you've ever hacked your way through is a battalion's payslips. You . . . fighting the Japs?? You couldn't punch your way out of an origami toilet-bag!

CURRY: You . . . you . . .

PHIL: And just what did you give me the boot for, anyhow? Wasn't for the cheek I gave you . . . we've all done that. And it couldn't've been for loafing about either . . . that's de rigeur in this joint. No . . . what got you by the short and curlies was the thought of me . . . scruff . . . going to the Art School, wasn't it? That I just might have the savvy to realise there was more to life than giving myself house-maid's fucking knee on them slabs!

CURRY: Shut it! Shuttit, you miserable young upstart! How dare you shoot your mouth off like that?? How dare you! Since the day and hour you walked through that door you've tried to caw the legs from under me. Yes, I wish it had been me that gave you your cards but Mr Barton beat me to the punch. "Get that lazy young bastard out of here, Curry, or I'll have those gaffer's stripes off you quicker than you can say 'Super Saxe Three-Quarter Square' ". Yes . . . that's knocked you back, McCann. Muggins here even asked for a second chance for you. Me! For you! So you go to your Art School and I hope it's a damn sight easier for you there . . . right?? And for your information Jimmy Robertson's got hammer toes. He couldn't even "Dig For Victory"! *(Exits)*

SPANKY: Plooky Jack and his plooky rush jobs. Wait till I get my desk . . . just wait!

PHIL: I wonder what the Guv'nor's got for one's tea t'night? Plate of jolly fine mince, perhaps? Or a shoulder of lamb to cry on? Best fling the leg over the trike and zip back to Fairyland . . . find out, eh? Confront the old duffer . . . break the news about the scribblin' school, the sack, and . . . oh, yes, the Old Dear's impromptu dip, what? Might stop off en route and chuck a bottle of bubbly in the boot . . . cheer the little tike up.
*(Picks up dustcoat)* Would you mind stuffing that down Quelch's throat as you leave, old bean? Thanks. Oh, and do pop a few of Bunter's boils for me, there's a good chap. Think I've got everything . . . ? Yes. Gosh, and All Serene, what a bally day. Started off pleas-

antly enough . . . one's Mater off for a few days in the country . . .
but, fuck me, if it ain't gone downhill since then. Fuck me, if it ain't!
*(Pause)*
Christ, I've just remembered something . . . *(Takes a couple of steps
and executes a cartwheel)* Giotto used to be a Slab Boy, Spanks!

*(Curtain)*

*The End*